# CORPUS ANIMA

Chiron Publications, 932 Hendersonville Road, Suite 104, Asheville, North Carolina 28803.

www.ChironPublicatons.com

ISBN  978-1-63051-365-8  paperback
ISBN  978-1-63051-366-5  hardcover
ISBN  978-1-63051-367-2  electronic

Cover illustration (detail) from
Horae ad usum Parisiensem, 1475-1500,
Bibliothèque nationale de France
(used with permission)
Black and white linocut images from
"The Wheel of Life " by Peter A. Ziermann,
Oakland, California 1986
Fernando Pessoa photograph (1914), Creative
Commons Attribution
Back cover photograph by Marian Dunlea  Book
design by John Hamilton Farr
Printed primarily in the United States of America

Library of Congress Cataloging-in-Publication Data

Names: Monte, Cedrus, 1949- author.
Title: Corpus anima : reflections from the unity of body and soul / by Cedrus Monte, Ph.D.
Description: Asheville : Chiron Publications, 2016. | Includes bibliographical references and index.
Identifiers: LCCN 2016011816 (print) | LCCN 2016014615 (ebook) | ISBN 9781630513658 (pbk. : alk. paper) | ISBN 9781630513665 (hardcover : alk. paper) | ISBN 9781630513672 (E-book)
Subjects: LCSH: Mind and body. | Jungian psychology. | Spiritual life. | Sacrifice.
Classification: LCC BF161 .M66 2016 (print) | LCC BF161 (ebook) | DDC 153--dc23
LC record available at http://lccn.loc.gov/2016011816

to all those who have been in my life I thank you
every last one of you
for the gifts and lessons
you have bestowed
for helping me to awaken
and come forth

especially my mother
gentle teacher, fearless warrior
for the common good


Mercedes M. Monte
December 23, 1922
July 15, 2015

# Corpus Anima

## Reflections from the Unity of Body and Soul

by

Cedrus Monte, Ph.D.

# CONTENTS

# THIS BOOK

The ideas in this book represent a significant part of my life's journey. This particular period started in 1980. The bigger journey started long before then of course.

The events that began to unfold in 1980 were, at least in part, a response to a dream I had in 1976. The dream: A vision of da Vinci's Vitruvian Man, arms and legs outstretched, standing in the middle of a circle and square, with words coming to me out of the dream ether: *All forms of expression need to be experienced in order to be truly alive.* I didn't know exactly what the dream meant at that time, but I knew it was important.

The Vitruvian Man is a drawing by Leonardo da Vinci from 1490. It represents the combination of art and science during the Renaissance. The picture also represents da Vinci's desire to illustrate the relationship between nature and humankind. Leonardo envisioned the human body he had drawn as a cosmography of the microcosm. He believed that the patterns and workings of the human body were analogous to the patterns and workings of the universe.

Whatever I had dreamt, I was being given some insight about the body, nature and the cosmos, and about their undeniable and inextricable relationship.

Consciously and unconsciously, I have ventured to live that dream. Doing so has included formal study in the arts; receiving teachings from Native American leaders and other spiritual teachers; instruction from psychotropic medicine healers, including peyote, psilocybin and LSD; studies and experiences in ritual theater, butoh, Reichian therapy, bioenergetics, transpersonal psychology, Jungian psychology, and more.

All of it has formed into my profession as a Jungian Analyst.

These diverse experiences were never a matter of dilettantism, but rather of living the dream I had in 1976. The dream pressed up from roots deep within me, from its own desire and longing to take form. All the explorations, studies and experiences mentioned here led me to the ideas expressed in this book. The table of contents is sorely incomplete in that regard, but the book is still at least a memoir of the traces, no matter how incomplete, of my journey.

All the experiences in my life so far were necessary to bring me to the central ideas in this book, which are the following: It's not an either/or world; it's a paradoxical place, this earth, where seeming contradictions are in harmony, and apparent opposites exist as true at the exact same second. It is a place where matter and spirit are indivisible, being of the same moment in time and space. Where the soul of the earth is one with and the same as the soul of all beings. It is a world where corpus — body — is ensouled; where anima — soul — is embodied.

It's a world where the Corpus Anima roams free, calling to us, full of longing and desire to show us all She knows.

Before it's too late.

Cedrus Monte
Zurich, Switzerland
2014

# Reflections

This chapter is a compilation of short writings made from May 2004 to March 2008. They were posted on my website under the title, *Reflections*. It is my feeling that some of my best writing comes in these short, poetic-prose pieces. They are like little seeds, some of which have taken root, some of which are still germinating. They are images that come from the sensing of the heart. Two of these entries were used in the published articles that follow. I decided to keep them here in the Reflections chapter as well nevertheless. They are particularly significant for me.

## Sunday, May 23, 2004
## The Anima Mundi in All Cells

My best friend took me to a new place the other day, and I knew I had to return. Something called. When I first arrived I thought, *This would be a good place to die, to just let go and allow my spirit to find release, let my body dissolve into the earth.* Something of that happened there this morning, though not as I expected...which is a good thing. I will try to explain.

The challenge for me has been to let my rational, conscious awareness be as subsumed as possible by the impulses of the natural world: to surrender my own smaller needs. I realized this morning, however, that I no longer have enough intelligence to do this. (I would risk saying that at one point, maybe twenty-five years ago, this intelligence was stronger in me, but over the years the need to be someone has made me dull.) I have tried to make myself available to the natural world, but I have become so dense, so filled with data and thoughts and expectations, the natural world has a difficult time finding a way in.

When I arrived this morning, I thought I would work on the "movement of dying." I had a plan, in other words. I would do this and this and this, and then this...which is, of course no real dying at all. Fortunately, I found a way out of this folly or, better put, a way out found me. This place that had called was, indeed, a good place. Soon, I was emptied into its presence.

Standing in the midst of the trees, they found a way in. There was no longer "me" trying to move. For a grace-filled few moments, the trees were moving me, speaking a kinetic, wordless text. By grace again, "my plans" to die deceased. Through the earth and into my feet old roots and long memories filled my limbs. A tempest storm raged. Mute cries of outrage and tortured screams. Whose memories were these? Whose tempest storm? Were these the trees speaking, or were these my own flesh memories unearthed and uprooted?

I believe the only answer to this question is, Yes!:

The place of trees was speaking the same speaking in me.

**April, May, June 2004**
# Landscapes of the Soul

*The following text was read at the beginning of one of the movement courses I have taught. It is meant to bring an expanding awareness to the nature of movement, the body and the world.*

How we conceive of ourselves, our bodies, and our bodies in time and space, define in part who and what we are. Down to the words and wording, to the languaging, is how we are determined and defined. How we move in the world, how we think, what we think, are influenced by how thought forms itself in the mind. If we think of ourselves, because of our languaging and our notions of reality, as an object moving through space in linear time, separate from other objects, then we set up an experience of object and subject with a limited understanding of time. We omit circular time, we omit eternal time, we omit the field in which all resides simultaneously and through which all is inextricably related. We omit zero, the void point, the absolute stillness out of which all arises.

The movement work attempts to challenge the experience of subject and object as well as chronological, linear time. Rather than, "I am walking on the road," we shift and we have, "Roadwalking is happening." Rather than, "I am singing a song," we have, "There is singing going on." (Thank you, F. David Peat.)

We can take one step further and say, "The song is singing itself. The walking or movement is moving itself." In other words, the song and the movement are living beings. The movement we invite is a being that we honor with our attention and our surrender to its expression. We offer ourselves to the impulses of the unconscious, temporarily sacrificing ego desires.

The more we conceive of the human body not as mechanistic, not as biological reactions, but as the physical manifestation of "fields of meaning" and "processes of knowledge," the more we will be open to subtle levels of energy, the subtle levels that are contained within the process of healing.

> [Physicist David] Bohm suggested that, in its deepest essence, reality, or "that which is," is not a collection of material objects in interaction but a process or a movement...of the whole. This flowing movement throws out explicit forms that we recognize through our senses of sight, smell, hearing, taste, and touch. These explicate forms abide for a time and we take them as the direct evidence of a hard and fast reality. However, Bohm argues, this explicate order accounts for only a very small portion of reality; underlying it is a more extensive implicate...order. The stable forms we see around us are not primary in themselves but only the temporary unfolding of the underlying

implicate order. To take rocks, trees, planets, or stars as the primary reality would be like assuming that the vortices in a river exist in their own right and are totally independent of the flowing river itself. (F. D. Peat, 1996, p140)

The knowledge or insight gained in this movement course is yours. It resides and springs from deep within. Once the experience is felt, it cannot be taken away. At the same time, you are the only person who can give the experience and the ensuing insight to yourself — by commitment to the process, by removing the critic, by dropping smallmind and letting your body become your field of perception. This takes practice, and it is practice that this work helps to provide.

### Thursday, May 13, 2004
## Moving in the Bardos

As you may have noticed on the Courses page of this website, I offer workshops in movement. This work has evolved out of more than thirty years of inquiry into the body. I am fortunate to have studied with some very fine teachers, some known and some unknown, either in classes or in long years of private, collaborative research. Each teacher and colleague has been an original pioneer, offering a crucible of discovery by way of their excursions into the unknown.

When I started a few years ago to offer my own courses on a formal basis, I saw very quickly how imperative it is to keep the work alive by direct and sustained participation in the process, either with a teacher or colleague or through self-designed inquiry. I believe we must find a way to feed ourselves if we are to help feed others. Otherwise, we soon starve.

This spring, I realized I was starving and had to find a way to sustenance.

After considerable thought, I knew I needed to do something that was immediate, alive, flexible, related to the organic, natural world. Taking my cue from Min Tinaka, Japanese *Butoh* dancer and teacher, I decided to go walking in the early morning to see what movement would arise spontaneously, just letting myself be formed and moved by any impulses I might experience while in nature. I mentioned this to a friend of mine who offered their support by sometimes walking with me and sometimes taking photos.

These first inquiries have taken shape by getting up at 5:30 in the morning and walking by the Limmat, the river that flows out of the Lake of Zurich, through the city of Zurich, and on towards Baden.

I had great expectations for myself, for the project. But I soon learned that the expectations bowed to "a lesser god," one of small moves and gradual, imperceptible changes.

Just getting up at that hour was a commitment of great effort: I was used to ending my day at two or three in the morning. At 5:30, my body was more like a piece of lead than anything mutable and receptive. I soon realized that just showing up, and letting myself feel all the resistance and discomfort it felt, was the exercise. Simplicity, humility, patience. Maybe, just maybe, I would be able to perceive something of the nature of river, stone and tree in the tiny quivers of cellular recognition and corporal mutuality.

There have been micro-seconds of this recognition. There have even been spontaneous arrivals of birds, according to my friend. Watching, according to my friend. Sometimes it really is only these precious micro-seconds of genuine receptivity to life that we are granted. Perhaps we can learn, with patience, humility and an open heart, to let the seconds move into moments.

**Friday, June 18, 2004**
# Flesh Memories

For years now I have experienced a place or a moment in somewhat Proustian fashion: A breeze moves past in a certain way, a certain scent arises in the air, and my body is flooded with a kind of memory, or a recollection...my body, not my mind.

The memory is often without visual image, but always with corporeal sensation...a kinetic image. Walking suddenly into a quality of air or sunlight stirs places in my body, flesh memories returning like a tender, caressing lover. A couple of days ago: raining, stepping onto the tram from Wollishofen to Central, taking a seat on the hard wooden chairs, suddenly being thrust back into time from the touch of the moist air, the movement of stepping up onto the tram, feeling the wood against my back. No visual memory, nothing specific to recollect cognitively, just a sudden journey back into time, or some parallel place.

Trying to pin down the memory is often to no avail. At that juncture everything disappears, memory, sensation, everything. I've learned to just let the feeling come in and to simply notice the quality of feeling, sometimes appearing in the heart or in the throat. Fleeting, though grace-filled. A Visitation. Perhaps an annunciation of some secret birth, a sacred child, the presence of whom vanishes under the stress and glare of demanding definition.

I am often under the strain of an existential angst, both personal and collective. These flesh memories are sweet "remembrances of things past," reminding me that there are times when life is actually joy-filled. These visitations seem to open the heart, diminishing the need for defense and protection, diminishing the demand to know intellectually. These flesh memories come from the unexpected, from the small and subtle. They allow me an open window into grace.

If I, if we, move too fast, want too much, too soon, these visitations can never be noticed. We rush past them in our relentless search for "The Big Prize." Next time you are curiously stopped in your tracks, next time you feel a hand has gently rested on your heart, or you feel the impression of some unknown remembrance, let that sensation in, let it unfold, let your body lead the way soundlessly into the mystery of that cellular Visitation.

To surrender into not knowing, into the mystery, requires us to become more attentive, to awaken, to invite and receive the silence.

Do not be afraid of the silence. It is full of what we need to hear.

**Friday, July 30, 2004**

## Numen of the Flesh

In his letter dated August 20, 1949, Jung says it is the numen which offers "the real therapy, and inasmuch as you attain to the numinous experiences you are released from the curse of pathology."

A brief description by Jung of numinosity might be appropriate here. He refers to the numen as "a dynamic agency or effect not caused by an arbitrary act of will. On the contrary, it seizes and controls the human subject...The *numinosum*—whatever its cause may be—is an experience of the subject independent of his will...The *numinosum* is...the influence of an invisible presence that causes a peculiar alteration of consciousness." (CW 11, par. 6)

Perhaps the visitation of the numen is mostly understood as a descent of the Spirit into flesh, a transpersonal visitation that floods the body and mind with its presence. An event in which this is celebrated, for example, is Pentecost, a commemoration of the descent of God the Holy Spirit to the twelve apostles, granting them the sudden and miraculous gift of tongues.

In contradistinction—not opposition—to this view, I would like to propose, as well, the possibility that the numen is contained by and released from the flesh itself, a presence indigenous within, *and as,* the material body.

By bringing psyche and soma into mutual focus, we address the full spectrum of the soul: archetype and instinct. It is my understanding that this can only unify and strengthen humanity, bringing it into greater relationship and harmony with the rest of the natural world.

**Friday, July 02, 2004**
# Flesh Memories II

Although I refer to flesh memories in the last entry as somewhat Proustian in that they often feel like memories of things past, they may also be forays into a parallel understanding, a concomitant reality where comprehension is purely instinctual, with the conscious mind simply along for the ride.

Or...

these flesh memories may also be, as James Hillman suggests in his book, The Soul's Code, a call from the soul already in full comprehension of our path, beckoning us to some understanding still secret to the ego.

Or...

they may be the flesh alerting us to deeper realities through pan-matter communication: electrons of one body — of air, tree, chair, stair, water or stone — communicating to the electrons of our own bodies, helping us make connections in new ways, enlivening a greater sense of eros.

And then again...

they may be all of the above. Real truths, I believe, express themselves in multiple ways, just as dreams do.

We can be stirred in so many ways, have the ecstatic experience of the flesh with all of life in the exchange of mutual recognition and praise.

Perhaps if we could grasp this understanding, truly grasp it, violence and war would be obsolete.

### Wednesday, August 18, 2004
## River River

I have come to love the Limmat River. It's the one mentioned earlier...the one that got me up at 5:30 in the morning to move with it. I haven't been as faithful to the movement as I had intended. But I have been faithful to the river. I go down to the river regularly, to be with it, walk with it. Being there does something to me.

French physicist, Jean Charon, talks about the nature of matter in his book, *The Unknown Spirit.* He speaks a great deal about electrons. His work has guided us to the discovery that our body's electrons enclose a space and time unlike the one we have so far assumed. In the electron space-time continuum, there is a memory of past events that continuously and endlessly empowers and enriches not only what we call our mind, but every single cell of our being, in the very electrons that combine to make us who and what we are.

He says electrons form the building blocks of all matter. All life is made up of electrons. Furthermore, he says these electrons communicate with one another, learn from each other, whatever the distance and whatever the species — human, non-human and otherwise. Electrons are able to exchange informational or spiritual (he uses these terms interchangeably) content with each other in the ever continuous flow of life's evolution. He goes on to propose that the electron is the wordless link between all of life, the bridge to inter-species and pan-matter communication.

Being a metaphysician at heart, I don't doubt this at all. I feel this, unequivocally, down by the river.

According to Charon, "As time flows, Spirit increases its order within each electron. It has no choice in this: it consists of a space in which order cannot decrease, a non-decreasing negative entropy space...The electron does not consider this constant negative entropy increase as an aim in itself, in other words the *object* of evolution, but as a means of *discovering the objective* of evolution...Each electron is like ourselves: as it increases its memorized information, it begins to perceive a new objective and to mould its actions accordingly...That is why we can speak of the spiritual 'adventure' of the universe, since Spirit is choosing to exist through constantly increasing awareness." (1977, p.167; italics mine)

I am not sure what happens to me at the river, but I do feel that I am heard. However, it is not this "I" that is heard. And I do feel that I can hear something. But it is not this "I" that hears it.

It's in the cells.

## Monday, September 13, 2004
## Not Everything Has a Name

To prepare you for encounters with inexpressible mystery, I offer you the following words of Alexander Solzhenitsyn, from his Nobel Prize acceptance speech:

"Not everything has a name," he said. "Some things lead us into a realm beyond words...to revelations unattainable by reason. It is like that small mirror in fairy tales—you glance in it and what you see is not yourself; for an instant you glimpse the Inaccessible, where no magic carpet can take you. And the soul cries out for it."

Entering the realm beyond words, being exposed to places unattainable by reason. Sometimes we are extraordinarily fortunate: We point our vision and see what we would normally see, but Someone, Something, offers it back to us in its REAL, ineffable form. We are struck with awe, with the numinosity of what has been hidden, but there all along. This is what happened last night...walking by the river.

**Tuesday, October 05, 2004**

## Pentecost of the Body

Perhaps the visitation of the numen is most often understood as a descent of the Spirit to humankind, a transpersonal visitation from "above" that floods the body and mind with its presence. An event in which this is celebrated, for example, is Pentecost, a commemoration of the descent of God the Holy Spirit to the twelve apostles granting them the sudden and miraculous gift of tongues.

In contradistinction—not opposition—to this view, I would like to propose that the numen is contained by and released from the flesh itself, that the numen is a presence within and as the material body. The flesh, the body, is not only the receiving vessel of the numen but, by the very nature of matter itself (as suggested by physicist, Charon), the body is also the generator for what Jung has referred to as the *numinosum*. By addressing the body, through the body, we have the opportunity to experience an alteration of consciousness that is available to us when we are grounded in somatic experience and informed by the numen of the flesh. We have the opportunity to free ourselves from what Jung refers to as the "curse of pathology" and to further our course of individuation...through the consciousness of the body.

**Tuesday, November 30, 2004**
## Dark Days and Times of Love

It has been quite some time since I've contributed anything to these reflections. November 2, 2004 was a Dark Day if ever there was one in American history or, should I say, world history. It took me days to recover from the election. I joined with millions of other people around the planet in a global depression. It was, and is, a time of mourning.

Many thoughtful writings have been offered, expressing a sense of outrage and sometimes hope. Since that time, and actually long before, I have continually asked myself what I can do to affect any kind of positive change. I am still asking myself. I do not have any definitive answers.

Robert Sardello, founder of the School of Spiritual Psychology, has suggested that this age of nuclear annihilation demands that we learn to love when we can find nothing to love. This notion has turned over and over in my thoughts, like a koan that brings us to another level of awareness. It has "saved" me (just barely) from despair, many times, realizing that my despair—or lack of love—brings me right to the place that can teach me the most about love.

Perhaps this is, indeed, one of the best things I can do: to learn to love when I can find nothing to love. With this ability (which I must renew each and every day, sometimes with each and every breath) I have a better chance of refusing to be used as fodder, eaten alive by the monstrous hatred, greed and fear that is overwhelming our world. Perhaps, with this ability, I am better able to bear the dissonance that threatens to rip us apart, body, mind and soul.

I often feel this near-ability is the only thing that keeps me alive. This, and the desire to bring into form that which is fueled by something greater than myself. Sometimes this ability manifests in (or as) the work I do with people. Sometimes it comes in the act of making an image—written, visual, kinetic. They can connect me anew with the sweetness and beauty of life that become invisible in despair.

Until I learn what more I will do, these efforts alone require great strength on my part. It is not quite enough, I know, but out of these efforts, perhaps something true can arise.

**Wednesday, January 26, 2005**
# Making Images

Image-making was for centuries a sacred act. It still is in cultures that keep these traditions alive. The following was written by someone who knew this. I no longer know who wrote it. I have kept it for almost 30 years, referring back to it many times like a touchstone for my own sensibilities. It reminds me of what real image-making is about; and it sums up my own quest in the area of making images.

East Indian aesthetics sees art in reverse from the way we do. We think that an artist has a brilliant idea and then independently executes that idea. But the creation of a Buddha icon, for example, is thought of as the Absolute descending into the world. The vision in the mind of the artist is the first stage of the descent. Then, using susceptible material in the relative world (paint, paper, clay), the Absolute impresses itself as form.

Meditation on this icon reverses that process. The viewer sees the form and then recreates the vision through the imagery. When it is realized that the image in the mind is not itself an object, the resulting experience — that is, of identifying with the immaterial — recreates the Absolute.

At that point, neither the icon nor the vision are required. The viewer is the Buddha.

The time is ripe for renewing this quest in my own way.

## Monday, March 21, 2005
# The Canary in the Mine

I often wonder if big, world events — like the U.S. invasion of Iraq — are felt as tremors in the collective psyche well before they manifest on the physical plane. Perhaps the tremors come as an increase in a collective dysphoria, with the whole of societies feeling jittery and disruptive for no particular or obvious reason. Then, suddenly, the event descends and there is some strange release—toxic, but with the feeling of relief for the dispersion of tension, followed by horror and grief.

For weeks now I have been feeling the possibility of this phenomenon. Is this my own particular psychic instability? An activation of my own complexes? Or is this the subliminal recognition of one of those collective tremors? Am I one of those canaries in the mine? Or am I simply unable to recognize my own unconscious contents? The probability is that it is both: I am both extremely sensitive to collective tremors, and I am always unearthing dark and heretofore secret treasures from my own private cache of complexes.

Those who are inclined to canaryism seem to tread perpetually on persistently active tectonic plates, with both physical and psychic ground constantly shifting beneath their feet. It is difficult, if not impossible, to feel secure, to feel that anything is permanent or sure. From some perspectives, this would warrant a diagnosis pointed toward pathology. From others, the start to lifting the veils of illusion. Whose perspective is best? Can we really say? If so, how?

Can we really say in these times of untold global upheaval that those who feel insecure, uncertain, marginalized beyond collective recognition, are those who need the most help? Or is it those who feel certain about where they are going and what they are doing, having achieved measured success in worldly (and sometimes even spiritual and psychological) undertakings, who most need the ministrations of counsel and reflection?

I believe we are living in an increasingly upside-down, inside-out world, where white is black and black is white. Do not fear your fears. Do not doubt your doubts. They are most likely quite warranted, and therefore very healthy. Those who are very sure often shoot first and ask questions later.

Have you been feeling mysteriously depressed and dysphoric lately?

**Tuesday, April 12, 2005**
## Shifting Ground

This is a confession.

When I came into adulthood—let's say in my mid to late twenties—I began to experience the ground shifting under my feet. Metaphorically that is. Before then, the metaphorical experience was there but, I would say, it was largely unconscious.

Living in California one might conjecture that the feeling was a result of strong sensitivities to lumbering tectonic plates. Having lived in various places around the globe since that time, however, I would have to say that the sensation of shifting ground has more to do with sensitivities to impermanence, of all kinds.

This sensation has never abated.

Quite honestly, I have had the persistent and nagging feeling that at some point "it" would all fall apart. That what we knew as civilization would in some strange way just disintegrate. On some very profound albeit unconscious level, what we were doing as a species never quite made sense to me. I wouldn't have been able to explain myself then (nor can I do so to my satisfaction now), but the inexorable movement toward power and having and conquering and progress never seemed to jive with the dance I was doing. I felt mysteriously and hopelessly out of step.

Quite honestly, again, I now feel that this internal, personal perception of shifting ground and the incredulity at our trajectory as a species is finally and unilaterally being reflected in the outer world. The madness created by the polarization of having and doing and conquering is in full sway...as never before. The news, especially the news emanating from the thrust of the one so-called super power, is horrifying and incredible. And yet somehow I feel that I am no longer "delusional." What I felt for so long from early adulthood (and probably childhood) can now no longer be denied. It does seem to be falling apart.

And for this, I am actually quite grateful.

Perhaps when and if our current structures do finally disintegrate, then and only then will we have the opportunity to contemplate our madness. And perhaps then and only then will we have the opportunity to see that those who have suffered the most, those who have suffered and broken down in mental disease, in emotional frailties and in physical weakness, were truly the sane and strong ones, carrying with all their strength and courage all that the rest of us could not even begin to bear.

## Sunday, May 15, 2005
# Home

Where do you go when you go back home? Do you have a home to go back to? A home place? I consider lucky those who feel this is possible. Other than the archetypal home that is always with us on the spiritual plane, internalized, immortalized within the realm of psychic reality, home seems to be more and more illusive. In the outer world.

For a wanderer and bridge-maker such as myself, home seems to be the place where I feel welcome, if only for a brief time: in companionship with the swiftly flowing river, watching the bones of trees flesh into green, and pink and white and lavender, or in the sweet company of a song bird who sings an if of day into yes! (Thank you, e.e. cummings!)

Home has become increasingly illusive to me. I truly miss the physical places that once were home to me in this world. The quality of air and sunlight. The caress of the sea breezes coming across the bay and up into the hills. As a child, when I was very sad or needed to be alone, I would climb up the ladder to the roof of the garage, where I could sit up against the upper trunk of the old fig tree in the backyard. Such a wonderful, old, loving and giving tree. She was home to me when I felt forsaken or needed to find myself again.

I think there is less and less real home left in this world. I don't mean to be negative or pessimistic, but as I mourn my own personal losses of home, I also mourn the loss of the reality of home in this physical world. There is something terribly wrong. Our home, our blessed vessel of earth and air and fire and water, is being devoured by the wolf of consumerism and profit and free trade and profit and more profit.

I wonder how much home we could give back to ourselves by letting go of our lust for having things. Always another car, a bigger and better house, yet another gadget. Every year. Every other year. Every six months. I wonder how much more whole and healthy and sound we could become by giving back to each other the true places of home: the health and beauty of the lands and waters and winds which sustain us.

I am sorry, dear friends, but I cannot help feeling that we are on the very verge of losing our home. Enjoy and love every bit of it, as much as you can, wherever you are, at any time of day or night, with all your heart and soul.

If nothing else works, perhaps, just maybe, this love alone can help return to us our Home Sweet Home.

**Tuesday, June 14, 2005**

# Too Much Too Many

Sometimes, actually quite often, I think there are just too many things. Too much stuff to deal with. Stuff. All stuff. In another lifetime I was, no doubt, a sadhu. I feel this sadhu wants to live again once more, within me, as me.

Even great thoughts are too many. Well, maybe there aren't *that* many really great thoughts. But there are certainly lots of books, and theories, and lectures and workshops and seminars and courses and more books and magazines and journals and newspapers and...blogs! (Let's not forget these blogs!) So many, many thoughts and ideas spinning around the earth. Spinning the earth. Spinning.

Sometimes the centrifugal force of this massive spinning is so strong, I just want to let go and fly out into the stratosphere. Into space. Into zero gravity. Silence. Complete and utter silence. Except for the music of the spheres.

Ah-h-h, Heaven!

I think sometimes that's exactly the thing to do. Let go. Completely. Stop the striving. Stop the spinning. Just STOP! And breathe and relax and be....*Nothing.* Nothing to do. Nowhere to go. Die 100% into the moment, after moment, after moment.

When was the last time you were able to do THAT!?

I dare you.

...Hah! I dare *myself!*

## Saturday, July 02, 2005
## Sticks and Stones Indeed Break Bones...

...but that is not the end of the story.

I believe in the beauty and elegance of the broken and the downtrodden. More than anything, I think. The strong and invulnerable, without those broken places, do not interest me...not unless it is a strength that comes from having suffered much.

Not only am I not interested in what is perfect, but I feel terribly uncomfortable in the presence of something that has not been in some way broken. Wounded. Where would my wound find true welcome otherwise?

The healing of the wound comes in this recognition:

What is vulnerable, broken, is of special and fragile beauty. And to that end, it is fully and deeply embraced.

If we cannot do this, if we cannot embrace the vulnerable, I feel we can never find peace.

**Friday, April 14, 2006**

# Return

It has indeed been a long time since writing anything here. It doesn't mean I haven't been reflecting, however.

Today is Good Friday.

I am often enlivened on Good Friday. Enlivened by the collective movement inward. It is a day when things become very quiet, at least in many predominantly Christian countries. Here in Zurich (and all of Switzerland for that matter), it is a full holiday or, probably better said, holy day. Almost all stores and businesses are closed.

Yes, I am enlivened by the collective movement toward quietude and reflection, or at least the semblance of it. Even if it is somewhat artificial, one can clearly feel the difference between a day like this and a day when it is all happening "out there." This is an inner celebration...of Death. And that, too, enlivens me—that a day is taken out of the collective calendar to acknowledge Death. How absolutely rare this is. And in it, I rejoice.

How could consciousness rise again and again, if it were not for this time of dying? How could we ever return if we did not first fade away into death?

Perhaps if we could really do this, acknowledge Death, we would not need to kill innocents, and innocence, to feel, erroneously, that we will prevail and survive.

To all those who have lost their lives in sacrifice to our inability to acknowledge the real meaning of Death, I bow in deepest respect and deepest sorrow. I also bow in gratitude. Their suffering is innocent suffering, just as Christ's suffering was innocent and, therefore, somehow redemptive—even if unconscious and unacknowledged.

To all those in Iraq and other places who are tortured, maimed and decimated by the shock and awe of Death's denial, I suffer with you.

May the consciousness of all soon be raised, enough to stop this madness.

## Tuesday, July 04, 2006
## In This Body

Kabir was a 14th century Sufi mystic and poet from Northern India. Listen to what he has to stay about the body:

### In This Body

In this body forests and hamlets, right here mountains and trees.
In this body gardens and groves, right here the one who waters them.

In this body gold and silver, right here the market spread out.

In this body diamonds and pearls, right here the one who tests them.

In this body seven oceans, right here rivers and streams.
In this body moon and sun, right here a million stars.

In this body lightening flashing, right here brilliance bursting.
In this body the unstruck sound roaring, streams of nectar pouring.

In this body the three worlds, right here the one who made them.
Kabir says, listen seekers: Right here my own guru!

and yet another....

## Where Did You Come From?

Where did you come from?
Where are you going?
Get the news from your own body!

It's all right here...if only we can stop and listen.

**Friday, September 22, 2006**
# A Deeper Love

I've known Peter Ziermann for twenty years. Most of the photographs on this blog were taken by him. Some of his art work is also included.

As artists, he and I stole from each other all the time. We were openly jealous of each other's work, wanting to claim it for ourselves. We soon learned it was our highest compliment to each other, this thievery and jealousy and covetousness. Because we respected each other's work, when these feelings were stirred we knew that what we had just done was good and had intrinsic value.

We reveled openly in these shadow elements.

This was and is one of the deepest expressions of love I have known, some of the grandest acts of generosity I have ever experienced. We did not deny our primitive desires. We used them to nurture each other into a deeper creative spirit, into spaces where we could give the best of what we had to give.

Living is much easier knowing that I have shared this with another human being. Dying will be the same: easier for having lived this.

I can imagine it might make many lives easier.

### Sunday, February 10, 2008
## The Clear Bead

Rumi writes:

> The clear bead at the center changes everything.
> There are no edges to my loving now.

I've heard it said there's a window that opens
from one mind to another,

but if there's no wall, there's no need
for fitting the window, or the latch.

Cultivating emptiness seems to be exactly the opposite
of what most endeavors in the world encourage us to
do. We try to fill ourselves up with so many things that
our minds burst and our bodies go numb. We
desperately try to be someone. Sincerely. We try
desperately and sincerely to be someone. For the
greater good, we say, this desperation and striving
serves.

If we have nice things, things that are coveted by the
many, we feel somehow that we are doing a good job at
being a success. Again, Rumi speaks:

Someone who goes with half a loaf of bread
to a small place that fits like a nest around him,

Someone who wants no more, who's not himself
longed for by anyone else,

He is a letter to everyone. You open it.
It says, Live.

Truly living and cultivating emptiness require
authenticity, a willingness to drop masks and pretense.
They demand true courage and humility, simplicity
and an open heart. Cultivating emptiness requires
living from the clear bead of the heart. If there are walls

around our heart, if our minds are jammed tight with what we are told is important to know, how are we ever able to open our hearts and minds to the other? How can we ever follow the movement of soul?

I wonder how different training programs in the psychoanalytic world would be if these principles were not only taught, but followed, if they were present not only in content but also in the day to day process of teaching and learning.

Clear beads are not generally encouraged, especially within endeavors involving power, prestige and a sense of elitism, like psychoanalytic institutes. Usually, the more you have the better it is. In my professional world this would mean more analysands, more articles published, more books written, more lectures slated. Always more. I'm not saying that these things are bad. But without a deep sense of consciousness about what drives us to these things, we tend to mistake having them for a sense of worth and meaning and accomplishment. We tend to put them between us and the other, creating a wall, a window, and a latch.

I wonder what the practice of analysis would be without the assumed power, prestige and elitism that accompany the profession.

I have heard repeatedly from others about the lack of genuine loving kindness, the lack of heart in the process of personal exchange within the institutional psychoanalytic setting. Indeed, I have seen this myself. I do not believe this way of acting is intentional, necessarily, but perhaps the lack of awareness about the nature of our interpersonal exchange is even more insidious and damaging than outright intention.

If it is not intentional then what are we doing?

As Otto Kernberg has said when writing about psychoanalytic institutions, it is not enough to bring our grief "to the hour," meaning it is not enough to take to one's analyst the wounds received from abuse of power and lack of sensitivity within the hierarchical structure. As long as the problem is treated solely as the individual's "shadow," this lack of true loving kindness and the inability to act from a place that is void of the will to personal power remains. As long as all players do not examine themselves openly and with ruthless honesty, genuine creative life suffers. The place and importance of process is denied. In a relatively self-contained hierarchical system it is easy for this to happen.

It is clear that these kinds of concerns are not exclusive to any one profession or group. I think we are all, individually and collectively, struggling to find the answers to these problems — to the loss of soul, the loss of our humanity.

**Friday, February 01, 2008**
# The Path Less Followed

The following comments arise from my own personal feelings and observations. They are not necessarily fact, nor are they necessarily true for anyone other than myself.

In the last few years I have felt quite strongly that there is something amiss in the practice of analytical psychology. It's not the psychology itself as Jung created it that I feel is problematic. Not at all. Rather, it is what I perceive to be the hierarchical institutionalization of training and practice. It is also the form of the practice itself that feels, for me personally, more and more out of Tao.

Interestingly enough, I have increasingly heard from other Jungians who feel the same as I do. They are flung far and wide across the globe — in Canada, America, Switzerland, Brazil, South Africa. I am sure if I were to continue speaking with other Jungians around the world, I would find many more in still other countries.

My sense is that there is a great need to address what I, and apparently others, perceive to be amiss in the Jungian world. And we would need to address our concerns within a form and a forum that does not perpetuate the same hierarchical and institutional approach. An alternative approach would embrace the creative, non-hierarchical, round-table democratic practices that are deeply aligned with what can be described as the feminine principle, a way of perceiving that is greatly marginalized in a hierarchy. The new approach for our inquiry might be far less organized and ordered, allowing for the spirit of the moment to usher in the necessary focus. It would also include the world at large, directly, palpably. We would not be listening to someone give a formal lecture standing at the front of a room, reading from a paper. We would not, necessarily, be following a leader in an experiential workshop. Inquiry and presentation would be live, in the moment, attuned to the central question.

When I say "feminine principle" I am not talking about women, or women's liberation or any other such thing. I am talking about the ability to be in relationship with each other equally, not hierarchically, placing greater value on process rather than product. I am speaking of an approach that embraces creative chaos, fosters the desire to receive each other through the heart, through eros, and to have every voice truly heard.

It might be nearly impossible to run an institute in these ways, but it is, to a large extent, what many of the Jungian training institutes profess as the centerpiece when working with the psyche, with the unconscious: we are instructed to follow the movements of soul.

The way I see it at this point, institutes do not, maybe cannot, practice what they teach.

## Sunday, March 16, 2008
# A Musing

There are many elements that distinguish Jung and his work. One of the most powerful forces in Jung's life was the impetus to re-create himself, again and again, old ideas constantly being reworked or replaced with the fecund muse of the moment. This force asserted itself in his life at the risk of death more than once, both physical and metaphorical. Jung was a scientist, yes. A mystic, definitely. (I have never thought that a pejorative term in relation to his work.) And an artist. He was an artist not because he painted or worked with stone, but because he was willing to risk death — rejection, ridicule, disenfranchisement, banishment, and loss of life — to find the truth of his life as the Muse wanted it to be lived.

Jung didn't want to have his work institutionalized, at least not in the beginning. I don't really know what changed his mind, but I doubt he was ever completely enthusiastic about codifying something that grew out of his particular relationship with the Muse.

Indeed, how can one write a procedure manual, complete with regulations and by-laws, that tells us how to wrestle with the Angel when we meet it on the road to the Unknown?

# Corpus Anima

# AT THE THRESHOLD OF PSYCHO-GENESIS

The following essay appeared in the anthology *The Moonlit Path: Reflections on the Dark Feminine*. Ed. Fred Gustafson. "At the Threshold of Psycho-Genesis/The Mournful Face of God." Nicholas-Hayes, Maine. June 2003.

The first chapter alone (that which follows here) originally appeared in *Quadrant: Journal of the C. G. Jung Foundation for Analytical Psychology*, New York, New York. "At the Threshold of Psycho-Genesis." Spring 2001.

*The secret is that only that which can destroy itself is truly alive.*

C. G. Jung[1]

## The Paradox

For some of us, if not for all, meaning in life periodically finds its way through a piercing and deadly darkness. Hopelessness and despair can descend like a toxic cloud, even in the midst of a joy-filled life, a life of spiritual discipline and intent, and dedication and commitment to conscious growth. Dark moments can strike like a sudden, rending eruption from mysterious and subterranean places. Without warning, the crust of a forever-healing wound, or an old insidious trauma is torn open unexpectedly, and we bleed again. We feel that we have entered into the abyss, body and soul. In the darkest of these times, nothing—no word, no prayer, no loving gesture, no therapeutic intervention—reaches the mark. Everything is lost, crumbled and gray, pointless—our life hopelessly flapping in the maw of a terrifying yet welcome annihilation.

How do we find our way through these darkest of spaces? Jettisoning a way out is impossibly dangerous, a too-heroic feat for this tenuous and precarious state of being. Remaining at this threshold of pain feels intolerable. And yet, given the grace of enough psychic ground, by staying with the intolerable dissonance we can once again restore our faith and experience the rare jewel of equanimity. Here, at an unfathomable but fecund threshold, something can change, something new can come forth.

Faith that arises at points of near-unbearable suffering is a faith born by sustaining absolute paradox. Those who endured the Holocaust and the devastating events of the Third Reich have been able to communicate the profound meaning and acceptance of this paradox and provide us with unprecedented teachings. Innocent suffering in the Holocaust, as in Christ's innocent suffering, has helped to redeem humanity's ignorance and lack of true compassion. The unparalleled gift of such understanding shows us how to survive trauma of inexpressible dimension. In testimony, in his *Letters and Papers from Prison,* Bonhoeffer writes:

> We cannot be honest without recognizing that we must live in the world "as if God did not exist." And so we recognize this—before God. God himself compels us to this recognition. So our coming of age leads us to a genuine recognition of our situation before God. God lets us know that we must live as those who get along without God. The God who is with us is the God who forsakes us... The God who lets us live in the world without the working hypothesis of God is the God before whom we eternally stand. Before and with God we live without God.[2]

Others have also offered insights, quickening to paradox as a means toward spiritual and psychic regeneration. Robert Sardello at the School of Spiritual Psychology suggests that the explosion of the first atomic bomb traumatized our consciousness as a planetary people. Considering this situation, Sardello reflects:

> The explosion of the Hiroshima bomb in 1945 opened the crust of the earth and created an entry into the Underworld for all of humanity. The anxiety provoked by this event—a mythic occurrence—has profoundly disturbed ordinary consciousness. It has completely separated human beings from past spiritual meaning and brought unresolvable unrest, leading to indifference and to a pre-occupation with comfort. That is to say, since

this event, ordinary consciousness has lost its meaning.

What is the soul's response? It is the quality of stillness. The soul becomes completely quiet, for it has entered into the realm of death…there to begin the task of learning how to be awake and fully conscious. It is a test. The aim of this test is to find whether the force of love, no longer arising from attachment to things in the day-world, can be born out of the soul itself. In other words, can love arise where there is nothing to love?[3]

According to Sardello, our task in facing the threat of total annihilation is to find a way to regenerate our world, both inner and outer, psychic and physical, through the power of love born not of existential security but of the inescapable presence of annihilation. Here, as well as in the example of Holocaust survivors, the presence of a lethal, traumatizing condition prompts and demands the emergence of an even greater vivifying force. A traumatic condition begs a bio-psychic genesis, an instinctive and spiritual arising of new life.

Finding new life through the profound acceptance of death is the paradoxical solution. In paradox, we stand at the threshold of life's resurgence. Holding fast the divergent reigns of painful dissonance, we enter realms of deeper healing.

# Sites Within Paradox: Hydrothermal Vents and The Black Madonna

## SITE ONE: HYDROTHERMAL VENTS

In 1991, a crew of marine biologists had the unprecedented opportunity to witness the birth of a deep-sea hydrothermal vent. Hydrothermal vents, originally discovered in 1977 in their advanced state of development, are one of the most toxic environments on the planet, emitting lethal concentrations of hydrogen sulfites. The vents arise through volcanic activity at the meeting place of the Continental Plates, known as the Mid Ocean Ridge, where the earth's crust is formed. Here, in the lethal environment of the vents, scientists have discovered extraordinary sites of what some consider to be bio-genesis, the spontaneous emergence of new life. At a depth of 8,600 feet, where there is no light for photosynthesis, new species of subterranean flora and fauna spontaneously arise in prolific numbers and thrive in the toxic environment through the process of chemosynthesis. Vent organisms are unique to their geography and their habitat. They are found in no other location. Since vents were first discovered, over three hundred new species have been identified, and every expedition discovers more. Speculation as to how vent life arises ranges from ideas about dormant larva ignited by the superheated water that follows volcanic action, to inter-planetary cross-fertilization from comets and meteors that have entered the earth's orbit. [4]

SITE TWO: THE BLACK MADONNA

In approximately A.D. 797. St. Meinrad was born of royal parentage in Central Europe. In 822 he was ordained as a Benedictine priest, eventually becoming a hermit six years later. Ultimately, his hermitage was founded as the Einsiedeln Monastery, which now lies within the borders of Switzerland, and is dedicated to the Black Madonna, the Virgin Mary. A universal phenomenon, the Black Madonna still lies within the sphere of mystery. There are an estimated 400 shrines to the Black Virgin, yet she remains little known, a subterraneous figure even within mainstream Catholic cosmology in which she is firmly rooted. As will be more fully explained below, the Catholic Church has little explanation for her blackness, except to surmise that the figures have been long exposed to candle soot and therefore darkened. Seen from a psychological and historical perspective, however, the Black Virgin is an archetypal figure of pre-Christian origins and has always been black. She carries the dark pole of the feminine archetype. As such, the Black Madonna is the religious expression of one aspect of the Godhead, revealing its dark, unconscious, mysterious and unpredictable side.

St. Meinrad's initial approach into the realm of the Black Madonna began with his hermit's journey, delineating the religious expression of his desire for greater intimacy with the unconscious or the Unknown. To establish a hermit's refuge, St. Meinrad traveled deep into a dense and virgin forest: the dark and mysterious aspect of the unconscious, the Black

Madonna in vegetative form. Soon after establishing his refuge, St Meinrad was confronted by an overpowering multitude of spectral demons that arose from the forest. To these fearful figures, he surrendered completely, lying prostrate in prayer and terror on the ground. After a long time, an Angel of deliverance appeared out of the east, and the demons were dispelled.[5] At the threshold of unpredictable and utter demonic destruction, a redemptive, fecund beginning presented itself. Through his prayerful surrender to the demons of the dark wood, St. Meinrad plumbed the darkest depths of the unconscious—existential terror and a sense of total abandonment—out of which new life, a new beginning, emerged. Here in the dark wood the hermit built the first edifice of what has now become a foremost point of pilgrimage to the Black Madonna. Like Bonhoeffer, St. Meinrad survived the trauma of God's abandonment, in and with God.

## SITES ONE AND TWO PARALLELS

In both situations above, new life appears at the threshold of trauma and destruction: volcanic eruptions generate toxic vents where bio-genesis occurs; and St. Meinrad's life-threatening confrontation with demons brings about a spiritual birth, an event of psycho-genesis. Hydrothermal vents present a biological correlate or analogue to the psychic reality represented by the Black Madonna. At vent sites, bio-genesis occurs in total darkness at the ocean floor, and lethally toxic material is transformed into fuel through chemosynthesis. In the realm of the Black Madonna, we plumb the depths of our being where we confront and transform the toxic psychic substances of fear, betrayal and profound uncertainty. As a result, we are presented with the opportunity for vital and creative growth.

Observation of toxic hydrothermal deep-sea vents and recognition of the archetypal nature of the Black Madonna may offer us vital clues for undertaking the soul task that Sardello proposes. In these examples we find that life, i.e., love expressed at instinctual and spiritual levels, can thrive in spite of, and even more importantly, because of, what formerly we believed would bring about a total absence or annihilation of life.

In the ecosystem of hydrothermal vents, life thrives and flourishes through symbiotic relationships where chemosynthesis takes place. The tube worm, for example, takes in hydrogen sulfite ($H_2S$) and brings it down into a large sac filled with bacteria. The bacteria then process the $H_2S$ and give the worm energy. The tube worm is able to detoxify a deadly substance by bringing it to its symbiont, the bacteria. A cooperative process breaks down and transforms a toxic substance into fuel for survival.

The Black Madonna has been compared to personages in other cultures and spiritual traditions, including Persephone of the Underworld, Kali, and Isis.[6] These are goddesses or deities whose rule lies within the dominion of surrender, death and rebirth. From the perspective of the ego, they are lethal forces. But without yielding to this composting and transcendent energy, no transformation is possible and therefore no renewal of life-force. As archetypal energies within the psyche, what these personages accomplish is the breaking down and transmutation of toxic substances, thereby fueling soul growth. Psychically toxic substances, like the hydrogen sulfites that originate deep within the bowels of the earth through volcanic activity, are primitive and primal energies which erupt into consciousness—fear, pain, pride, rage, envy, our intolerance—which can be converted into fodder for spiritual regeneration. Primitive energies become transformed not by denying them, but by working them into new life through heightened consciousness; that is, by fully acknowledging them, as St. Meinrad acknowledged the spectral demons of the dark wood when surrendering himself in full prostration on the earth. Only when we are willing to fully and deeply acknowledge the presence of these dark forces can the Angel—our redemption—come.

## Darkness and the Imago Dei

The Black Madonna is revered in many shrines and cathedrals of Western and Eastern Europe. She has existed there for centuries. It is only from the middle of this century that the Black Madonna has been present in the United States, the figures of which are descended from the Virgin at Einsiedeln in Switzerland.[7]

The darkness of the Virgin is enigmatic. Different sites of the Black Madonna offer different stories for her blackness. The story within the tradition at Einseideln describes the original figure of the Madonna as needing restoration when long-standing candle soot had accumulated on the white skin of the Virgin. Gustafson, in *The Black Madonna,* includes a first person account given in 1799 by Johann Adam Fuetscher, ornamental painter and restorer. Fuetscher states that the statue of the Madonna he received for restoration was blackened by intensive exposure to church candles, but that beneath the soot was white, flesh-colored skin. Cryptically, and without explanation, he notes that in his restoration, *he painted her black,* that is, as the statue had appeared when originally it came to him for restoration. He does not say why his restoration is to black rather than white, flesh-color. He goes on to say that over the black pigment he painted in eyes and some color for cheeks and lips, but that when the statue was viewed by church members they firmly requested that she be painted completely black, thus requiring Fuetscher to paint over the eyes and other areas on the face to which he had lent a rosy color.[8] Clearly, in her darkness, the Madonna gave something to her petitioners that she could give in no other form.

Marie-Louise von Franz offers another explanation for the Madonna's blackness, one that encompasses the archetypal and pre-Christian dimensions of this special figure. Von Franz explains that statues of the Black Madonna, including that of Einseideln, were always black, being original descendants of the Egyptian goddess Isis and her child Horus, who in the Late Roman Empire played an important role. Wherever the Roman Empire spread, the Isis cult rooted; and there you find statues of the Black Madonna. She goes on to say:

> ...what is stressed about Mary is her spiritual aspect — the Immaculate Conception, the Assumption into heaven into the heavenly Thalamos or bridal chamber — but Isis had a much richer theme. Isis was represented as the highest divine spirituality, but she was also worshipped as the underworld goddess, ruler of the dead....Isis was a black goddess...nocturnal, earthy...She was a mother goddess who comprised, or contained in her image, the highest spirituality — she is the Mother of God, the new sun god Horus, and wife of the reborn Osiris — and also the darker chthonic aspects of the Great Mother. She unified them all....The Virgin Mary inherited those traits, but in the official teaching she inherited only the sublime and spiritual, the attributes of purity and so on. The other aspects, of earth fertility and the dark side, were never officially recognized.[9]

Given the people's response to the restoration of the Black Madonna at Einsiedeln, it seems apparent that the official church image of the Virgin was incomplete. The people, then, provided necessary compensation for the Virgin's incomplete state in their request for a completely black skinned Madonna and Child.

Whatever the explanation for the Black Madonna's presence, apparently it is the very blackness of the Virgin that gives special hope to those who come to her. She is able to encourage and sustain those who seek her certain solace precisely *because* of her darkness. Within the nature of her being, she holds the paradox: in and through darkness lies a fertile resurgence of life. No doubt, it was the reassurance of this experience that people fervently sought by having her returned to her blackened state.

The presence of the Black Madonna fulfills a collective need within the psyche. Her presence informs us that we can, and must, fully embrace the darkness of the unpredictable and unknown. While a thrashing torment may accompany the hopelessness and despair of a profound rupture in our connection to what we know, exactly at this juncture a penetrating vision of faith, and new life, comes into being.

The *Imago Dei,* the image we have of God, is not only what we, from our *egoic* stance, perceive as good. As Bonhoeffer and Sardello explain, we must open wide enough to believe in the goodness and love of God, even when we can perceive no good or loving God in which to believe. As the fecundating and dark side of the feminine Godhead, the image of the Black Virgin helps us to endure and survive this dilemma, born of piercing and deadly uncertainty.

As a counterpart in the natural world, bio-genesis at hydrothermal vents gives precedent to the psychically regenerative nature of the Black Madonna. It presents an apparently impossible yet living paradox: in the most lethal environment—in chemicals more toxic than deadly cyanide, under the crushing weight of water that measures five thousand pounds per square inch (enough to liquidate a tank), at the junction of near-freezing deep-sea waters and volcanic vent-waters reaching up to 750 degrees Fahrenheit, in pitch-black darkness where no photosynthesis is possible — plants, spaghetti worms, sea dandelions, orange sea stars, crustaceans and a litany of others spontaneously arise and thrive. Indeed, new life forms manifest and proliferate as abundantly as on any coral reef found in the ocean. On this point scientists agree: through vent life, a new vision of the world is brought to light. An event of this magnitude cannot be ignored or left fallow, neither in the outer world of nature nor, by analogy, in the inner world of the psyche.

Vent discoveries have prompted interdisciplinary scientific approaches which are mutually focused on the possibility of global detoxification and the discovery of new medical remedies. Greater understanding of the archetypal dimensions of the enigmatic Black Madonna may direct us to similar resolutions at the level of the psyche, both personally and collectively.

# The New Vision: The Threshold of Psycho-Genesis

St. Meinrad's experience in the forest when confronted by spectral demons describes the daunting nature of an intra-psychic, depth-psychological journey often referred to as *The Dark Night of the Soul,* or *The Night Sea Journey.* In this inner journey, one plumbs the depths of a spiritual *nigredo,* mining a possibly more profound sense of faith. Comments made by marine biologists and other scientists about the experience of their adventures and discoveries in relation to hydrothermal vents are remarkably parallel to the nature of this journey into the deeper layers of the psyche. C. G. Jung's pioneering observations on the nature of the personal and collective unconscious aptly define these subterranean realms in psychological terms. One method by which he describes these realms is by comparing the maturation of the individual personality and the development of consciousness to alchemical processes found in ancient texts on Alchemy. In the alchemical opus, the true beginning of the journey commences when the "matter" turns black. One alchemist writes, "When you see your matter going black [in the alchemical retort], rejoice: for that is the beginning of the work."[10] By comparison, Jung postulates that getting to a state of psychological wholeness means—at least for starters—confronting our own blackness: pride, greed, envy, fear, alienation. Without this first step, we cannot find true light, the inner gold.

In addition to facing a personal experience of darkness, one fundamental task in applying Jung's analytical psychology in our own lives is to open to the mysterious and often terrifying depths of the unknown, and through it to an experience of the *numinous,* to the touch of a transcendent force. Through the grace of the *numinous,* the transcendent enters our lives and brings us to a new level of consciousness. Only then do we find the inner gold of which the Alchemists spoke, a condition of which is referred to here as psycho-genesis. The journey through the unknown to wholeness is no ordinary journey. It requires unending courage and willingness to endure what often seems impossible to bear. An experience of the *numinous* arises not only from ecstatic-filled light, but just as often from the mournful darkness of isolation and despair.

The following comments are made by vent explorers. One could make the same or similar comments about the perils, and ultimate riches, of *The Night Sea Journey*, the psychological dimension of the alchemical *opus*:

There's no template for this research. Most of the work here has to be newly engineered…

The abyss is no normal laboratory…

The trip to inner space [deep sea waters] in many ways is more treacherous than a trip to outer space. The pressures are enormous…

Each trip [down to the ocean floor] is an opportunity to discover previously unknown life. It is a slow trip, but one brimming with excitement…

You travel down…through the inky blackness of the deep sea and you get to the bottom and you see this growth of life. There's [sic] thriving communities. There's so much activity going on. It's like no place else in the universe.

Each and every dive we find something and discover something that we've never, ever seen before...

One of the real challenges of working in the deep sea, and one of the reasons it's so exciting to us, is it probably represents the most extreme environment on the planet, particularly when we're dealing with hydrothermal vents.

Our appreciation for how little we know about life on Earth has really been manifest since the discovery of the vents...

Within all creation myths of the world, the *Imago Dei* brings new life into existence. In considering our present "creation myth" of hydrothermal vents, the possibility of bio-genesis transpires even under the most lethal conditions. As vessels of the divine spark, it is also our nature to bring new life into existence through the development of the psyche into fuller and greater consciousness. This hard-won development necessarily includes an acceptance of death. Death itself brings us to a fuller experience of life, not from the standpoint of the ego, but from the standpoint of spiritual growth, where we surrender our smaller will to the mystery of the Unknown. A full acknowledgment of death prompts us to the procreative possibility of bringing new soul life, a deeper love, into the world. Those like Bonhoeffer who have experienced extreme trauma with a profound understanding of what they have endured, found their way to an unfathomable faith which grew from an incomprehensible abyss of demonic chaos and destruction. Their spiritual legacy is a beacon to the world, their innocent suffering a redemptive act for the collective. In our day to day lives we, too, are confronted with the challenge of redemption whenever we are overcome with a personal experience of trauma, or a sense of alienation and despair. Bio-genesis in the toxic environment of hydrothermal vents reflects, in the natural world, the possibility of a psycho-genesis generated by accepting, and transforming, toxic sites of our personal experiences of darkness.

## Epilogue

After years of living a life of growing consciousness and simple spiritual devotion, one would think that the path of life becomes easier to navigate, that an inner light will radiate at the flick of a switch. This is not my experience. Nor, I am convinced, is it the experience for many other people of similar circumstances. Only by grace have I been spared the personal and direct experience of horrific traumas—natural catastrophe, personal holocaust and genocide. Yet, by the very fact that I am alive and therefore not without wounding, I am vulnerable to the periodic visitations of a quietly eruptive and deadly darkness, to the terrifying chaos of complete uncertainty.

Experiences of despair and loss of connection—even after breakthrough, life-changing events, extensive analysis, and a profound sense of communion with the forces of nature and spirit—have led me to believe, and growingly accept that my own path leads me repeatedly on pilgrimages to the inner shrine of darkness, not because I am morally deficient, not because I am depressed, and not because there's some form of enlightenment or personal maturation that I am just not "getting." Rather, I am led to the shrine of darkness because, in spite of a desire to consistently experience the peace and happiness of a certain spiritual liberation, the mournful face of God abides within me and wants to be seen, and loved, through my eyes. At this shrine I have learned to love when I experience nothing to love.

## REFERENCES

1. *Psychology and Alchemy. Volume 12. The Collected Works of C. G. Jung.* Translated by R.F.C. Hull. Bollingen Series XX. New Jersey: Princeton University Press, par. 93.
2. *Letters and Papers from Prison.* (1981). Dietrich Bonhoeffer. Macmillan, 145-6.
3. "Soul Tasks of the Coming Age." Robert Sardello. (November/December 1992). *Common Boundary,* 42.
4. All references to hydrothermal vents are taken from official transcripts: *Deep Sea Deep Secrets.* September 1998. *www discovery.com.*
5. *The Black Madonna.* (1990). Fred Gustafson. Boston: Sigo Press, 2-3.
6. bid. Chapter 4.
7. Saint Meinrad Archabbey. St. Meinrad, Indiana. *www.saintmeinrad.edu/friends/history.htm*
8. *op. cit.* Fred Gustafson. (1990). Boston: Sigo Press, 41-42.

9.  *The Cat: A Tale of Feminine Redemption.* (1999). Marie-Louise von Franz. Toronto: Inner City Books, 40.

10. *Mysterium Coniunctionis. Volume 14.* The Collected Works of C. G. Jung. Translated by R. F. C. Hull. Bollingen Series XX. New Jersey: Princeton University Press, par. 729, n. 182.

# Numen of the Flesh

The following article originally appeared in *Quadrant: Journal of the C. G. Jung Foundation for Analytical Psychology;* New York, New York. Summer 2005.

*For one who has spent so much time in the Absolute, perhaps embodiment and reconnecting with instinct and feelings is the resurrection.*

course participant

## Overview

The numen, according to Jung, is that which offers the real healing. Following Jung's lead, I propose that the flesh, the materia of the body, contains its own capacity for generating the numen, and therefore the experience of healing. The numen arises out of the flesh as a direct result of the very nature of matter itself. In other words, there is no split between spirit and matter. Every natural system has an inner life, a conscious center, from which action is directed. The body, the materia of the flesh, is one of these natural systems.

The collective unconscious contains not only the residues of human evolution but also the residues of animal evolution. Coming to terms with the unconscious—that is, becoming conscious—requires, therefore, a coming to terms with one's instinctual, animal nature. Given that one's instinctual nature is directly related to the body, one can propose that a new relation to one's body must be established for a more complete individuation.

Though Jung was deeply concerned with the question of instincts, the body itself was and continues to be largely marginalized in psychoanalytic practice. Wilhelm Reich, colleague of Freud and Jung at the turn of the last century, was the only real proponent of somatic inquiry, of working directly with, on and through the body. Unfortunately, he was rarely taken seriously. He was often mocked and sorely excluded from the formulation of psychodynamic understanding within the context of analysis and the unconscious. It is to Reich that many of the body-oriented approaches to the psyche owe their debt of existence, including Reichian therapy and bio-energetics. From the perspective of analytical psychology, this important work still remains in the shadows.

Considering the negative, pathological effects generated by the relative split of body and mind, it feels important if not imperative to offer skillful ways and means of affirming the irrevocable and harmonizing relationship between the instinctual, animal body and the archetypal, spiritual impulses of mind. To begin this task, I first offer a brief discussion on the nature of numen and matter. This is followed by contributions from participants involved in the somatic work I conduct. Finally, I include personal observations from my own somatic experiences.

## Numen

In his letter dated August 20, 1949, Jung says it is the numen which offers "the real therapy, and inasmuch as you attain to the numinous experiences you are released from the curse of pathology." (Jung, 1973, 8/20/49)

Jung refers to the numen as "a dynamic agency or effect not caused by an arbitrary act of will. On the contrary, it seizes and controls the human subject….The numinosum — whatever its cause may be — is an experience of the subject independent of his will….The numinosum is the influence of an invisible presence that causes a peculiar alteration of consciousness." (Jung, 1989, Par. 6)

In addition to the qualities listed above, the experience of the numen carries with it a fateful sense of meaning. It is not just a random or superficial experience but, as with the phenomenon of synchronicity, there is an understanding that the experience carries particular and personal meaning. One gains insight, often profound insight. Most frequently, insight and numen are one. Both are accompanied by experiences of surprise, shock, wonder, awe; both leave us feeling different in our skin.

Perhaps the visitation of the numen is most often understood as a descent of the Spirit to humankind, a transpersonal visitation from "above" that floods the body and mind with its presence. An event in which this is celebrated, for example, is Pentecost, a commemoration of the descent of God the Holy Spirit to the Twelve Apostles granting them the sudden and miraculous gift of tongues.

In contradistinction—not opposition—to this view, I propose as the main thesis of this inquiry that the numen is contained by and released from the flesh itself; that the numen is a presence within *and as* the material body. The flesh, the body, is not only the receiving vessel of the numen but, by the nature of matter itself, the body is also the generator for the experience of the numinosum. By addressing the body, through the body, we can experience the "peculiar alteration of consciousness" that is available to us when we are grounded in somatic experience and informed by the numen of the flesh. We have the opportunity to free ourselves from the "curse of pathology" and to further our course of individuation through the consciousness of the body itself.

## The Nature of Matter, the Nature of Flesh

### Glimpse I: The Electron

What is it about matter, including the matter of body, that would inspire such thinking, that is, the notion that the numen is contained in and released from matter or flesh? In his masterwork, The Unknown Spirit, physicist Jean Charon attempts to answer such physical and metaphysical questions.

Charon's work has guided us to the discovery that all life, including our own bodies, is made up of electrons. In this electron space-time continuum, there is a memory of past events that continuously and endlessly empowers and enriches not only what we call our mind, but every single cell of our being, in the very electrons that combine to make us who and what we are.

To this end, Charon explains that electrons, examples in particle physics of the "building blocks" of life, are able to exchange informational or spiritual content with each other in the ever-continuous flow of life's evolution. He portrays the electron as a veritable micro-universe. In this micro-universe, phenomena take place with what is called increasing negative entropy, that is, electrons continually increase their informational or spiritual content. In Charon's words:

> As time flows, Spirit increases its order within each electron. It has no choice in this: it consists of a space in which order cannot decrease...The electron does not consider this constant increase as an aim in itself, in other words the object of evolution, *but as a means of discovering the objective of evolution*...Each electron is like ourselves: as it increases its memorized information, it begins to perceive a new objective and to mould its actions accordingly...That is why we can speak of the spiritual 'adventure' of the universe, since Spirit chooses to exist through constantly increasing awareness. (italics mine) (Charon, 1977, p. 167)

Charon cites as further proof for the spiritual character of the electron the ability of the electrons to form systems with other electrons without any external help, as well as to develop hierarchical orders of ever higher complexity through increased information. Charon claimed that his research into the physics of elementary particles showed that electrons have the ability to store information, that they have a system of remembering and retrieving such information and that they communicate and cooperate with other electrons to create and operate complex systems.

All life is made up of electrons, speculating this as the reason for some people's recognition of their ability to communicate with all of nature, both animate and inanimate. In Charon's view, it is the electron that seems to provide the wordless link and language between all creation:

> An electron feels the electrostatic influence of another electron whatever the distance between them…Similarly, spiritual interaction between two electrons will be possible whatever the distance. (Charon, 1977, p.64)

Two quantum objects, therefore, once they have been in contact with each other, may be separated by light years, yet if one of the two objects reacts to being measured or observed, the other one, even though light years apart, instantly knows of the transaction and reacts by exhibiting a similar reaction. This fact has been called "inseparability of the quantum object" and has been experimentally verified beyond any doubt.

Finally, Charon believes the electron's journey is our journey, and that this journey goes out into infinity:

> We usually call this principle of infinity or eternity, God [the Infinite]...So, for the electron populating the universe, and also for us, the spiritual adventure of the universe is a search for God. (Charon, 1977, p. 168)

In the language of this presentation, we might say the very nature of matter, the very nature of flesh itself, is the drive for the experience and expression of the numen; here, making a direct link between "God" and the numinosum.

## Glimpse II: The Cell

The following comments, like the ones just previous, are of necessity abbreviated. I am not offering scientific evidence, rather a scientific metaphor. To that end, the second example suggesting the numen as a presence indigenous within and as the material body is found in Deane Juhan's classic book, *Job's Body: A Handbook for Bodywork,* where he reveals the enormously complex physical and extra-physical systems of the body and the relationship to the psychodynamics of psycho-spiritual health.

Juhan cites recent research made by contemporary biologist Candace Pert. Her research on cell receptors has launched the ongoing discovery of a wide variety of cell membranes whose functions take in and release information, as opposed to food or toxins or other such substances. This information dramatically alters the internal activities of the cell and its functional relationship to the rest of the body. (Juhan, 1998, p. 363) The discovery of cell receptors completely changes the understanding of cell function. It is now understood that rather than merely substances exchanged between cells, there is also information (or spiritual content) exchanged as well.

Pert has called these receptors "tiny eyes, or ears, or taste buds," sensory apparatus that provide the cell information for proper action in relation to the organism's needs. The receptor transmits information "from the surface of a cell deep into the cell's interior, where the message changes the state of the cell dramatically...and can translate to large changes of behavior, physical activity, even mood." (Juhan, 1998, p. 364)

The bonding of particular receptors with cells initiates the experience of a certain feeling state. Moreover, research shows that if the cells of an animal which has experienced a certain feeling state is injected into another animal, the same feeling is incited. These affects include sadness, disgust, anger, joy, fear, surprise. They all appear to have their individual and respective receptors. Pert asserts that these affects are not just the more familiar ones such as fear and anger, or states of pain and pleasure, hunger and thirst. In addition to these measurable and observable emotions and states, she also includes intangible and subjective experiences such as spiritual inspiration, awe, bliss, wonder and other states of consciousness of which we have all had some experience but that have been, up to now, physiologically unexplained. (Juhan, 1998, p. 367-8)

This suggests that there are specific receptors which stimulate or correspond to numinous experiences. Within the cells of flesh, there exists a physical, instinctual dimension which corresponds directly to the archetypal experience of the numen.

Receptor cells, then, can communicate the numen in the form of bliss, awe, wonder and other similar states of consciousness. In addition, within the cells, within the flesh, is the experience as well as the ability of the experience to "transmigrate," to be communicated from one separate entity to another. These are the instinctual dimensions of the archetype mediating the arising of the numen, coming not from "above," but from within and in direct exchange with the material, vegetative substance of life:

What is also fascinating is that the effects of the receptors are not...exclusively human. All mammals, in fact all species so far observed, have exactly the same...molecules. They are present in creatures that do not even have nervous systems, and indeed are the messengers that even single cell populations use to communicate with each other and organize the collective activities of the colony. Perhaps this is why so many people achieve such a deep and evidently mutual emotional connection with a pet...and why some individuals have such immediate rapport with creatures of all kinds. (Juhan, 1998, p 367)

We share with all of creation, the instinctual impulse to exchange information, including that of the ecstatic and awe-inspiring.

## Electron, Cell, and Numen: A Summary

In the examples of electron and cellular receptor, is the essence, the activity, the conductor and the delivery of the numen. In other words, it is the nature of matter itself to embody and transmit the numinous experience. The numen is within the flesh as the flesh, and accessible to us if we allow ourselves the opportunity to discover it. What we might call spiritual content or information, and what is referred to as the infinite, is accessible directly through and as the physical body. Within the paradigm of quantum physics this idea has been described as the notion that every natural system has an inner life, a conscious center, from which action is directed and observed. This is an animism that goes beyond participation mystique and brings us into the world of mystics and a shamanism that has become conscious of itself.

Because it is the nature of the electron to continuously increase in consciousness, the nature of matter itself is the desire to be opened to the influx and integration of the unconscious, of the Unknown. The nature of matter, and therefore the body, is the desire to conduct the Infinite. When the body is understood in this way, it can unfold us into the embodied Self. The body wants the experience of the numen because the numen is the very thing that is the center and core of its existence.

## A Personalized View of the Numen in Matter

Before presenting individual commentaries from movement participants in relation to this thesis, I would like to introduce a physiological view of the nature of flesh and movement as background to the work I undertake with individuals and groups.

### Connective Tissue: Piezoelectric Crystalline Molecules

The somatic experience is sometimes encountered in hands-on bodywork, sometimes in and through movement. In both cases the flesh is moved. From the discussion that follows, one might speculate that it is the movement of flesh that can deliver the insight, that carries the numen.

In *Job's Body*, Juhan devotes an entire chapter to connective tissue. Juhan states:

> ...its "connective" qualities cannot be overstated. It binds specific cells into tissues, tissues into organs, organs into systems, cements muscles to bones, ties bones into joints, wraps every nerve and every vessel, laces all internal structures firmly into place, and envelopes the body as a whole. In all these linings, wrappings, cables and moorings it is a continuous substance, and every single part of the

body is connected to every other part by virtue of its network; every part of us is in its embrace. (Juhan, 1998, p. 63)

Connective tissue belongs to a class of crystalline molecules called piezoelectric, piezo having the Greek root meaning "to press" or "to squeeze." Piezoelectric crystals generate spontaneous electricity when they are affected by pressure or movement. This considered, the entire matrix of connective tissue is "an electric generator producing fields of current whenever pressure or movement is taking place." (Juhan, 1998, p. 359) This energy production is what generates heat, keeping connective tissue pliant and all parts of the body in healthy relationship to all other parts of the body.

Connective tissue is also a semi-conductor of the currents they are generating. Semi-conductors are different than pure conductors. Semi-conductors are the various electrical mediums we use to transform electricity into other forms of energy and information. Heating coils, for example, use electricity to transform it into warmth; bulb filaments use electricity to make light; and phonograph needles (piezoelectric crystals) transform electricity into impulses that are amplified into sound. The web of connective tissue, then, does not simply generate electrical energy; it converts this energy into various forms, one of which is information. Connective tissue can be seen as a processor of electromagnetic signals informing one part of the body about another.

There has been much investigation on the biological significance of this piezoelectric phenomenon. (Juhan, 1998, p.359) Research has shown that every movement in the body generates electric fields induced by the compression or stretching of bones, tendons, muscles. These processes lead to pulsating fields that spread through the body. It is now assumed by some that the communication of information between various tissues and cells is, in part, generated and mediated by the electrical fields produced by the piezoelectric effect pulsing through the network of connective tissue.

In relation to the above phenomena and to the thesis of this paper, we can ask: What, exactly, happens when we engage the body to access greater consciousness? What does that mean? How does the numen become activated and released through the body? How does insight arrive through the flesh? From the discussion above, it is understood that the nature of flesh is such that movement is responsible, in part, for the dissemination of life-giving information from one part of the organism to the other, from one set of cells to the next. Movement, both autonomous and self-regulated (as in walking and jumping), or imposed from without (as in massage or other forms of somatic manipulation), is required for the continuation of our existence. Without movement, there is no life. Without movement or vibration, the spirit does not circulate. Without movement the numen of the flesh is not activated. Down to the smallest imperceptible vibration within the cell, the circulation and continuation of life is conducted through movement.

It would follow then that to gain insight in and through the body, one must let themselves have a fully-embodied experience, one must let the flesh be moved, as awkward and as disturbing as that can sometimes feel. What is required, according to this argument, is an "experiential study in movement."

## Experiential Studies with Movement Participants

In order to access the numen of the flesh, the stage must be set to invite and receive the insight available when it arises through the body. The proper context in which to receive insight, to be open to the numen, must be introduced. Bodybuilding, typical athletics and other forms of competitive sport do not set the context (though experiences of the numinosum have, in fact, been noted in martial arts, yoga and endurance sports such as long-distance running). In the West, the given context to receive insight through the flesh is largely defined within the parameters of body-oriented approaches to the psyche.

The following contributions from participants in body-oriented approaches to the psyche may help the reader to see in more detail how insight and numen can arise from the flesh. Although words rarely do justice to the true depth of feelings, they still remain one of the best ways to communicate any shifts in awareness or consciousness that occur.

To give an idea of the physical and philosophical context in which these experiences have taken place, a brief introduction to the movement/dance discipline of *Butoh* stands as a preface. The somatic work referred to in this writing has taken place within the context of many movement approaches including bio-energetics, ritual theatre and dance/movement therapy; however, *Butoh* has had the strongest and most pervasive influence. It is to *Butoh* and to those who have created and defined *Butoh* that I owe a great deal in the formulation of my current work.

## *Butoh*

*Butoh,* also known as Dance of Darkness, is a Japanese dance form that emerged out of post-war Japan which includes the experience of nuclear holocaust. Although its roots can be found in the oldest Japanese folkloric traditions, *Butoh* recognizes influences from post-war European movements, most predominantly, German Expressionism. Although one can make attempts to describe *Butoh* according to these categories, conclusive classification is not possible. *Butoh* arises outside convention, outside form, outside any prescribed approach. It is, at its most authentic, a protest against those very elements.

*Butoh* has been viewed by some as a search for a new identity, a way of establishing meaning for a society that had unmercifully experienced a profound breach in their personal, cultural and existential reality. It is considered by its practitioners to be an exploration into the unconscious, into the realm of imagination and shadows. Movement in this art form does not focus on depiction, nor is it choreographed in the usual way, i.e., shaping movement from the conscious level. Movement intentionally begins and continues from the inner recesses of the psyche. The focus is on tracking the immediate metamorphosis of psyche through movement. The discipline in tracking the psyche in this way can then, when desired, be ritualized or formalized into performance.

In *Butoh*, the intention is to follow, through movement, an internal psychic image to the conclusion of becoming the consciousness of the image itself. You are no longer moving like a river, for example, you become, as closely as possible, the consciousness of river. This approach encourages an experience of the primal energies which animate and nourish the very core of our being and engages the instinctual level of soul.

One well-known *Butoh* performer, Min Tanaka, traveled the entire length of Japan, dancing each day. His idea was to feel the difference in the ground at different places. He called the experiment Hyperdance. He said that the dance is not in the place, rather the dance is the place:

> The *Butoh* dancer tries to capture subtleties of the soul, understanding that dance is the movement of the soul…accompanied by the body. The soul is not there for others to like it. It is there to express what it has to express…The only requisite [for *Butoh*] is to not lose faith or hope; to pursue dreams and grab them strongly in the body, like a beautiful treasure that keeps us alive. Once there, it begins to

wake up and move the world of emotions and feelings. (Website: see References)

## Personal Accounts

The accounts included here are not case material in the typical sense. There is, therefore, little or no interpretation or personal background given. The participants have offered something of what was significant for them. They are snapshots of a much greater continuum of experience, starting from before the person arrives to the work and continuing on after the work is over as deeper reflection arises. The experiences offered are meant to give the reader an idea of how body, movement, sensation and kinetic image coalesce into an event or events that call forth sudden insight, or the numen of the flesh, and of how that experience can release an individual from the constraints which inhibit psychic growth. (Permission to use this material has been granted by each contributor.)

## Rafaela

In the following account, Rafaela describes her process as it unfolded. In this particular group session, we worked on the archetypal energies of Home and Exile, the point being to know through movement and the consciousness of the body what these states are, and to gain insight into the personal meaning of these themes.

The first stages of the somatic sessions involve physical warm ups, including running, bio-energetic exercises and other forms of movement. This is to open the body, encourage group trust, release inhibition to moving and, most importantly, to bring the center of consciousness into the body itself. In the second stage of the sessions, we work with material from the unconscious, either in the form of dream images, psychosomatic symptoms and/or collective archetypal themes such as Longing, or Home and Exile.

Each session is five hours long. Rafaela's account of the second stage of this particular session refers to the event that included walking back and forth across the full length of the room with all the other participants simultaneously, each holding a small piece of cotton about twelve by three inches in dimension. The cotton cloth is held between one's two hands which are extended straight out in front of the individual. At no time are the elbows to slacken in their extension. The only alternative position that can be taken is to raise the arms over the head, elbows unbent. The very slow, sustained walking and the holding of the cotton cloth is maintained for about thirty minutes. The exercise challenges our resistances, allowing something new to enter that cannot be controlled by ego demands. It is out of this physical challenge and strong discomfort — the physical equivalent to the psychic "holding the tension" — that something new often arises.

HOME AND EXILE: Rafaela's entry from her journal:

HOME: I chose a place in front of the window. The previous exercises had me centered and meditative enough to get in touch with the feeling of home (as opposed to what it looks like). The light poured in. The birds were singing, and the far-off sound of people's voices could be heard. Light and Beauty and Connection to the Universe through the sounds of people and nature. I felt the right to be here in this space and time.

EXILE: This was a killer. I'm not used to suffering pain and exhaustion in these kinds of workshops. And yet it worked, i.e., something happened that surprised and enlightened me about me, and that simply doesn't happen for me in other workshops. Also, what happened wouldn't have happened without the actual physical pain. We were to go through the exercise imagining that we were in Exile—a perfect juxtaposition to the last exercise of Home which made it an even deeper experience. No one we knew, no place to be, no one to help, only to keep walking and be in exile. You are alone.

Stage One: Walking back and forth and back and forth with arms straight out or up, elbows locked, hands holding unyielding cotton band. My self-talk: Can this be right? Am I doing it right? Is it supposed to hurt so much? How can I do this? I'll just have to do it because everyone else is doing it. I have no choice. I'm not allowed to quit when I'm on view. I can only quit in privacy because it's so shameful to quit/give up/fail. I can't opt out. I would once again fail to be engaged due to my

personal pain and anxiety. If they can keep going, I
guess I can. So I started walking fiercely—with
controlled Fuck-It Anger which fueled me because
no one and nothing else was going to be able to do
it for me. I was against it, and all I had was myself
and Fuck all of you.

Stage Two: I KNOW THIS FEELING! This thought
came as a total unbidden surprise. The physical
pain during that exercise evoked the same
emotional response that the emotional pain of
aloneness in my life evokes. Finding that out meant
something. It gave a new meaning to, or at least a
clearer picture of, my emotional pain. It's that
feeling when I'm in the depths: I'm alone. No one
connects with me, loves me, supports me, wants
me. I am not wanted. Given a lifetime of dealing
with it, I know how to get through it. The Fuck-It
energy is the only thing to crack me out of my
paralysis.

Stage Three: (This was about ¾ of the way
through.) All of sudden, I had a thought, again
unbidden: What if I can do this without the
extraordinary fierceness, tense body and rigid
laser-like anger? There must be a way to do this
without expending so much energy, without feeling
so miserable. So I let go of the anger and yet stayed
in the same focused energy place and became one
with the task. I stopped fighting and went with it.
Amazing! I could have kept going much longer—
pain got put in its place. It was like I was floating.

When I finally stopped and put my arms down, it felt AMAZING.

Stage Four: We were to go back Home. My final surprise. As I approached the spot in the room that was Home, as I came round the corner, I became overwhelmed with sobs and I collapsed. It was the contrast between the incredibly deep pain of Exile and being alone, and having a place where I had a right to be. I was home. I was Home.

---

Rafaela says she measures her connection to the Self by how deeply she is surprised by the experiences and insights she might have (in the movement work). This sense of surprise is, I feel, directly related to the arising of the numen. Surprise of this nature is sudden, pervasive and alterative, not within the control of the ego, and effecting an immediate shift in one's understanding. This brings to mind Jung's description of the numen noted above as "a dynamic agency or effect not caused by an arbitrary act of will." To the contrary, he says:

It seizes and controls the human subject...The numinosum — whatever its cause may be — is an experience of the subject independent of his will [generating] a peculiar alteration of consciousness. (Jung, 1989, Par. 6)

Grounded through her insights of the flesh, beyond a largely intellectual understanding, Rafaela found a new way to hold her sense of aloneness, her sense of personal Exile. She also found a new relationship to Home and to the way one can be in relationship to the world. The experiences will hopefully deepen and continue to serve her in the release of psychic energy which when blocked keeps us in bondage to the unconscious energies of our deepest complexes. When one experiences psychic energies in this way, when one is struck by the numen that arises from within the flesh, one begins to understand that what we are seeking is already within us in a very real, concrete way.

*Christopher*

When I think about the movement work I remember so many instances when, suddenly, what felt like an inner light started to vibrate through all the cells of my body. It was a kind of energy that went beyond my individual being. I felt linked to the cosmos. Often this light started to vibrate after the opening ritual. Later, I often thought that creating a sacred time and a sacred space and then starting to move is the perfect invitation to the numinous. It was somewhere in the room. It was somewhere in the cells of my body. Many experiences, even when they were painful, had a certain light in them. Often this light started to vibrate just when the pain was nearly unbearable, when the experience brought me into contact with sensations or feelings I wanted to dismiss as soon as possible. But the more I was able to go into the experience with all my awareness, the more I was available to a sudden shift in consciousness or understanding.

I am aware of how significant the movement work continues to be after the actual experience. That understanding comes in the form of what I call "body metaphors." It's like finding a very old and deep wisdom…in the body. These body metaphors have helped me in difficult moments afterwards, when they suddenly popped up involuntarily.

For example, this tiny little exercise: Starting with one hand closed and one hand opened and then, taking a full five minutes, you slowly, slowly, slowly open the closed hand while simultaneously closing the opened hand. Seems to be nothing special, but when doing this exercise for the first time, I thought I would never be able to move my hands again. I felt my hands didn't really belong to me. They seemed to be like stones, moving in an impersonal way and within the dimension of millennia. I felt a flood of panic starting to rise from deep in my body. I had to breathe in very focused way and not resist the experience. Then suddenly, the fingers on one hand made a jump; they moved, not smoothly, but with a jump, followed by a jump from the other hand. And slowly, the body awareness in my hands came back and I was able to proceed with the exercise.

Later, I realized that this experience felt very close to the experience I have when I'm emotionally blocked, when I'm not able to move forward or backward. I realized that it's exactly these jumps I need to come out of my blockage. Furthermore, I understood that I block myself with my own expectations of moving in a very gentle, tender or smooth way. I have to jump and to trust the unknown. I have to jump even if it doesn't look very graceful. And so this tiny little exercise has become a body metaphor for me that pops up involuntarily whenever I need it. And it has given me a lot of strength and courage to move on—to jump!

———————————

Each person who does this exercise has his or her very own unique experience of it (accommodating for some similarities). In Christopher's hands the psyche sought and brought the insight described. For someone else, the insight would be different.

What was it that electron, receptor and connective tissue coordinated for this insight to occur? Christopher was able to make the jump…yet how? Perhaps insight dawned as information gathered in the electrons, encouraged by the pressure of movement within the piezoelectric nature of connective tissue, making a leap, a "jump" in spiritual information. How exactly these things happen will probably remain a mystery. That they happen seems evident.

## *Anna*

When I first saw Anna in the group, I had a very strong and visceral impression. She was extremely quiet and contained, to the point of feeling painfully withdrawn and in a protective shell. Her hair was short and "practical." She was dressed in a very conservative and "proper" way. I had an immediate response: Will this work be too overwhelming for her? Will she derive any benefit from it? Will she leave in the middle if she is overcome with affect? I could only be very attentive and trust that we would find our way with each other, and she with herself.

At the end of the course, after witnessing her within the events given for exploration, I felt I had failed her. I was certain nothing had happened for her. She had come and received nothing; and there was nothing I could do. The surprise came when she wrote to me about two months later. This is part of what she said:

> I recently underwent a series of neurological tests to determine the cause of inadequate response to stimulus to my feet and lower legs. The tests revealed lesions in the white matter of my brain, and some deterioration in the discs of my neck and lower spine. The neurologist came up with a physiological explanation for my balance disorder, and told me I shouldn't worry. I was left with a feeling of vague dissatisfaction and the thought that perhaps there is more to this than can be technologically determined. What I do know is that this condition comes and goes. As I get older, it is

with me more than it used to be. However, I notice that increased physical exercise, even just more walking, results in almost immediate improvement.

Anna continues by explaining some of her experiences in the movement work:

> Several things happened which seem important. The dream image I worked with was that my knees wouldn't work when facing a serious threat. This is a recurring dream image from my childhood. When I became the dream image, I felt stuck and immobilized. I was also keenly aware of the emotions being expressed all around me [referring to other participants in the group], and wished they would go away. Once, I opened my eyes and thought of leaving, but I couldn't. Then, when you told us to be the opposite of the image, the best I could do was walk around in a circle with very small steps. When I thought about this afterward, I realized that I had been so limited and confined. I was unable to ask for help, or scream, or crawl away. This dream image is a metaphor for the way I deal with life. I can't cry out, I can't ask for help, I can't move in response to emotional threat.
>
> Since the work we have done together, I have given much thought and energy to a long-cherished plan I have to move to the country; I have also gained insight into a major guiding principle in my life. It became clear to me a few

days ago that I have been willing to go to extreme lengths of personal sacrifice in order to feel connected emotionally to a person or group. I can't quite explain why, but this insight along with the movement work has given me the information I need to mobilize myself and make the necessary changes to move to the country and live more for myself, and more fully.

------

I do not know the final results of Anna's neurological examination or what has happened since she contacted me; however, it seems that Anna's expressed desire to mobilize herself toward a life that would allow her to live in a way more responsive to her vital needs, to her soul needs, was the beginning of necessary change. By connecting somatically to the fear and immobility within the dream image, Anna was better able to understand, in an immediate way, to what extent she had been holding herself back.

This insight was precipitous; and it came from her relatedness and connection to her body within the vessel of the somatic inquiry or "exercises" provided. I had given her no interpretation, only an opportunity to engage in the experience and a willingness to acknowledge the numen of her insight. The understanding came from her, from her own body, from the flesh itself; from the ability of the flesh to support and contain the insight required to release her from a destructive immobility. The more she moved, and the more she was moved by her own insight, the more mobilized she became.

## Landscapes of the Soul Embodied: Personal Reflections

How we conceive of ourselves, our bodies, and our bodies in time and space, define in part who and what we are. Down to the words and wording, to the languaging, is how we are determined and defined. How we move in the world, how we think, what we think, all are influenced by how thought forms itself in the mind. If we think of ourselves, because of our languaging and our notions of reality, as an object moving through space in linear time, separate from other objects, then we set up an experience of object and subject with a limited understanding of time. In so doing, we omit circular time, eternal time, we omit the field in which all resides simultaneously and through which all is inextricably related. We omit zero, the void, the absolute stillness out of which all arises.

The movement work I do attempts to challenge the experience of subject and object as well as chronological, linear time. Rather than, "I am walking on the road," we shift and we have, "Roadwalking is happening." Rather than, "I am singing a song," we have, "There is singing going on." We can take one step further and say, "The song is singing itself. The walking or movement is moving itself." In other words, the song and the movement are living beings. The movement we invite is a being that we honor with our attention and our surrender to its expression. We offer ourselves to the impulses of the unconscious, sacrificing ego desires. (Thank you, David Peat.)

For years now I have experienced a place or a moment in somewhat Proustian fashion: A breeze moves past in a certain way, a certain scent arises in the air, and my body is flooded with a kind of memory, or a recollection...my body, not my mind.

The memory is often without visual image, but always with corporeal sensation...a kinetic image. Walking suddenly into a quality of air or sunlight stirs places in my body, flesh memories returning like a tender lover. A couple of days ago: raining, stepping onto Tram 7 from Wollishofen to Central, taking a seat on the hard wooden chair, suddenly being thrust back into time from the touch of the moist air, the movement of stepping up onto the tram, feeling the wood against my back. No visual memory, nothing specific to recollect cognitively, just a sudden journey back into some time, maybe fifteen years ago, maybe forty years ago. Perhaps both. Perhaps neither.

Trying to pin down the memory is often to no avail. At that juncture everything disappears: memory, sensation, everything. I've learned to just let the sensation come in and simply notice the quality of feeling, sometimes appearing in the heart or in the throat. Fleeting, though grace-filled. A visitation. Perhaps an annunciation of some secret birth, a sacred child, the presence of whom vanishes under the stress and glare of demanding definition.

I am often under the strain of an existential angst, both personal and collective. These flesh memories are sweet "remembrances of things past," reminding me that there were times, and could be still, and indeed are, when life is joy-filled. These visitations open the heart, diminishing the need for defense and protection. They come from the unexpected, from the small and subtle. They allow me an open window into grace.

If I, if we, move too fast, want too much, too soon, these visitations can never be noticed. We rush past them in our relentless search for The Big Prize. Next time you are curiously stopped in your tracks, next time you feel a presence in your heart, or you feel the impression of some unknown remembrance, let that sensation in, let it unfold, let your body lead the way soundlessly into the mystery of that cellular Visitation.

Although I refer to flesh memories as somewhat Proustian in that they often feel like memories of things past, they may also be forays into a parallel understanding, a concomitant reality where comprehension is purely instinctual, with the conscious mind simply along for the ride. Or, these flesh memories may also be, as James Hillman suggests in his book, *The Soul's Code,* a call from the soul already in full comprehension of our path, beckoning us to some understanding still secret to the ego. Or, they may be the flesh alerting us to deeper realities through pan-matter communication: electrons of one body — of air, tree, chair, stair, water or stone— communicating to the electrons of our own bodies, helping us make connections in new ways, enlivening a greater sense of

Eros. And then again...they may be all of the above. Real truths, I believe, express themselves in multiple ways, just as dreams do.

We can be stirred in so many ways, have the ecstatic experience of the flesh with all of life through the exchange of mutual recognition and praise. Perhaps, if we could grasp this understanding, truly grasp it, violence and war would be obsolete.

# Epilogue

It seems imperative for reasons that span the spectrum from spiritual and environmental health to the consideration of world peace, that we engage the integration of psyche and soma in ever greater earnest, not just by talking or writing about it, but by embodying it. With a more embodied sense of the self/ Self we have the opportunity of bringing our animal nature to the fore consciously and, as has been suggested, to further the deeper evolution of our individuation. We have the opportunity to realize a deep communication with all of creation. Holding this understanding in the flesh encourages the full-bodied sense of compassion and relatedness required to give consciousness a solid stand in the world. It allows consciousness the opportunity to be related, in the body and of Eros.

## REFERENCES

Charon, J. (1977). *The Unknown Spirit: The Unity of Matter and Spirit in Space and Time.* London: Coventure Ltd.

Juhan, D. (1998). *Job's Body: A Handbook for Bodywork.* Barrytown: Barrytown, Ltd.

Jung, C. G. (1973). *Letters.* Ed. Gerhard Adler, Aniela Jaffe; trans. RFC Hull. Princeton: Princeton University Press.

Jung, C. G. (1989). *The Collected Works 11.* Ed. Sir Herbert Read, Michael Fordham, and Gerhard Adler. London: Routledge.

Butoh reference:
*http://www.artandculture.com/cgi-bin/ WebObjects/ACLive.woa/wa/movement?id=891.*

# Corpus Anima

# The Body and Movement in Analysis

This essay was first published in *Jungian Psychoanalysis: Working in the Spirit of Carl Jung*. (2010) Ed. Murray Stein. Chicago and La Salle, Illinois: Open Court Publishing Company.

*When an individual has been swept up into the world of symbolic mysteries, nothing comes of it; nothing can come of it, unless it has been associated with the earth, unless it has occurred when that individual was in the body…. Only if you first return to your body, to your earth, can individuation take place; only then does the thing become true.* (C. G. Jung, Visions Seminar, 1313-14.)

During my mid-twenties I entered an impasse. Although I was far from being crippled, I could not stand for more than 15 or 20 minutes without experiencing debilitating pain. To counteract the exhaustion, I slept for hours during the day. The doctor finally suggested an operation to fuse the vertebra of my lower back. This was clearly not an option for me, so I began researching different modalities of treatment. Eventually, someone told me about a little known approach called Rolfing, a method of physical manipulation developed by Ida Rolf (1990). In those days, there were only about 30 Rolfers in existence, all trained by Ida Rolf herself. Today, Rolfing is practiced world-wide.

After the series of treatments, I was structurally and psychologically different, very different. Among many other changes, I stood straighter, naturally, becoming taller by almost an inch; without effort, my head rested differently on my torso; my shoe size changed considerably with my feet widening, allowing greater contact with the ground; and most importantly, I no longer experienced pain, a condition which has remained to this day, decades later.

All the energy used to uphold the structural imbalance and withstand the pain was now released, available to propel me forward into life. I felt the ground beneath me as never before; I could stand more readily on my own two feet. I had the energy and strength to meet the world and was eventually able to develop and promote my own work as an artist. In Jungian terms, one might say that the negative complex around which nearly all my libido had been focused was addressed to the extent that I became less regressively bound, constructively aligned with my own individuation process, no longer at such odds with who I was and with how I could serve in the world.

Soon after I was Rolfed, I entered Reichian therapy, a somatically-oriented psychoanalytic approach developed by Wilhelm Reich. Although Reich was a colleague of both Freud and Jung, his work was largely ignored. During the two-year period of my Reichian therapy, the unconscious was approached using the combination of direct hands-on address of body armoring as well as the psychological insight that is part of Reichian work. I was able to understand the deeper psychological significance of the process that unfolded. Most significantly, I became an active participant in the process. I became increasingly sensitive to what was happening physically in my body, at the same time learning to understand the psychological dimension of my feelings and bodily sensations. What I experienced somatically was the mirror image of what I experienced psychologically. As the armoring in my body gradually released, so did the regressive pull of psychological wounds that kept me armored and self-protective.

In time, my somatic explorations as a patient began to shift into somatic training as I continued to seek out and engage other ways of working, including approaches that do not necessarily require direct, hands-on manipulation. These approaches include exercises that employ the weight and positioning of the body as leverage for releasing body armoring and increasing the flow of energy in the body. They also include ways of embodying, through movement, imaginal material from the unconscious such as dreams, waking images, archetypal energies and psychosomatic symptoms.

During the same year I was Rolfed, I was introduced to C. G. Jung's writing. As is the experience for so many, I was deeply touched, his words giving shape and life to what had until that time lay unformed in my own mind. It would not be until some 15 years later, however, that I would enter Jungian training in Zurich where I began to interweave Jungian psychology with my work as a visual artist and the psycho-physical realm of the body. Well into my training, I also encountered the work of other Jungians involved in body-centered analysis, including that of Joan Chodorow (1991) and Marion Woodman (1996).

I have been asked by some, "Do you work with the body in your sessions, or do you work analytically?" From my experience, there is no dichotomy between the two, between working with the body and working analytically with the unconscious. This is not just a theoretical idea. As the reader might understand from the personal story I have shared, it is a deeply felt, experiential knowing of the spirit-matter continuum Jung so carefully traced in alchemical literature and which became pivotal in his work, including his understanding of synchronicity. From my own perspective as an analyst, the "soulwork" that analytical psychology offers can only be fully entered through the experience of the body-mind, psyche-soma unity, a unity that can be understood as the territory itself of the analytical opus. Any separation of body and mind, soma and psyche, in this context is artificial and unnecessarily divisive.

Before describing elements of a somatic, body-centered session, I would like to introduce two points the reader may find useful to understanding how I view the body within analytical psychology. The first discusses the transference; the second, quality of movement.

# The Transference in Body-Centered Analysis

Traditionally, the transference in analytical psychology is formed between the analyst and analysand at conscious and unconscious, knowable and unknowable, archetypal and personal dimensions of interaction. Additionally, an important aspect of the transference describes the analyst as "holding" the inherent whole-making, or S/self-healing of the analysand, mirroring it back to the analysand until he or she is able to claim and integrate the whole-making process more readily and more independently.

The same is true for a body-centered Jungian approach. There are, however, from my perspective, notable differences, described in part by the following.

Assuming that individuals are open to working somatically, it is possible for them to gain insight and understanding of unconscious material directly through the body. Even at the beginning of the work, this can take place without the intervention of interpretation from the analyst. This is only possible, however, as a result of the analyst's direct experience of bodily-triggered insight through his or her own personal work. Only then can the analyst encourage the analysand to grow in trust and confidence regarding what is offered up somatically.

I understand this somatic offering as the wisdom of the body, otherwise expressed as the Self contained within the flesh, as the flesh itself (Monte), the experience of which becomes a vehicle for rebuilding and strengthening one's experience of wholeness. Working somatically, the Healer archetype—initially transferred or projected onto the analyst—can more readily become embodied in the analysand. Through direct understanding at the instinctual, bodily level, insight is more fully the analysand's, thus engendering a greater sense of autonomy from the outset. An individual can retain the memory of inner experience more readily than outside interpretation. To this end, accessing bodily knowing can become an immediate resource for positive support and psychic sustenance. We discover that we can rely on ourselves more readily. We learn that we are able to access knowing through the ever-present resource of our own body.

We know what we know because we have experienced it in the flesh of our own being, not because someone has told us it is true.

The transference phenomenon in body-centered analysis or other forms of psychotherapeutic bodywork can, therefore, move quite readily from the interaction between analyst and analysand as primary or ultimate, to bodily experience as the medium which can reflect wisdom, self-awareness and the experience of Self. In other words, the transference field can shift from the interaction between analyst and analysand to a more intra-psychic exchange—that is, between the analysand's experience through the body and the ensuing self-reflection. The analysand relies far less on interpretation from the analyst and is, rather, encouraged to give voice to somatic experience and, most importantly, to the meaning of that experience.

Thus, there is a turning from the more hierarchical approach with the analyst as "the one who knows," to an approach that fosters direct, instinctual wisdom—the somatic Sophia.

## Movement as a Vehicle to and from the Unconscious

It is often the case that in dance and dance-like movement one expresses a feeling, an image, or a sensation; for example, sadness, sitting alone by a river, deadness or rigidity. Since the images provided by this kind of expression are quite often recognizable, one is given a comfortable frame of reference. While this approach is by no means to be excluded from the repertoire of a body-centered analytical approach, the broader idea of movement, for me personally, lies in deeper layers than the expressive one.

In deeper layers, movement is no longer employed in the body to express an image; rather, movement arises in the body as a result of being impressed and moved by the image.

To enter this realm one needs to trust enough, one needs to risk the perceived terrors of entering the darkness of what is not known. Put differently, one allows somatic impulses to momentarily take over without trying to devise a way to express or to control what emerges. When we can empty ourselves of preconceived ideas about how we should move, we create space to receive an impression or impulse from the unconscious. We can allow ourselves to be guided into the movement's own meaning.

Further, the movement becomes that which is being moved. It is not a representation of it. It is not a pantomime. We become, in our physical being, the image from the unconscious: You dream of a door opening.... How is "a door opening" experienced within you, as you?

When speaking about dream images Jung says, "Image and meaning are identical, and as the first takes shape, so the latter becomes clear." (Jung CW 8, para. 402) The impulse or image in the body, in movement, also carries its own meaning: as the movement unfolds, the meaning becomes clear. For this to happen, however, one needs the willingness to be moved, to surrender one's ego long enough to be pierced by the visitation from the unconscious in impulse and movement.

As I experience it, accessing the wisdom of the body lies in the ability to listen and to let ourselves be moved by something greater than ourselves. We no longer move our ego, but we are moved by that which moves us. Only when we wait, without being attached to outcome, can that which longs to be born from the unconscious be birthed.

To help illuminate these ideas, I offer the following journal entry from personal somatic explorations:

The other day, my friend took me to a new place in the forest. This would be a good place to die, I thought, to just let go and allow my spirit to find release, to let my body dissolve into the earth.

The challenge for me has been to let my rational, conscious awareness be as subsumed as possible by the impulses of the natural world, including my own body. I have come to realize, however, that I scarcely have enough intelligence to do this. I would risk saying that at one point, maybe 25 years ago, this intelligence was stronger in me, but over the years the need to be someone has made me dull. I have become so dense, so filled with information and thoughts and expectations, the natural world has a difficult time finding a way in.

When I returned to the forest this morning, I thought I would work on the "movement of dying." I had a plan, in other words. I would do this and this and this, and then this...which is, of course, no real dying at all. Fortunately, I found a way out of this folly or, better put, a way out found me.

Standing in the midst of the trees, they found a way in. There was no longer "me" trying to move. For a grace-filled few moments, the trees were moving me, speaking a kinetic, wordless text. By grace again, "my plans" to die deceased. Through the earth and into my feet old roots and long memories filled my limbs. A tempest storm raged. Mute cries of outrage and tortured screams. Whose memories were these? Whose tempest storm? Were these the trees speaking, or were these my own flesh memories unearthed and uprooted?

I believe the only answer to this question is, Yes!:

This place of trees was speaking the same speaking in me.

## Analytical Body-Centered Work in Practice

Somatic exploration in individual sessions can take many forms. Perhaps a dream has very strong images that beckon. It is also possible to explore certain archetypal, polar-opposite energies particularly germane to the mover: depletion/ vitality, creation/destruction. An embodied exploration of polarized energies can often yield a "third" element arising unexpectedly and surprisingly to inspire resolution.

In the sessions and courses I conduct there is no specific method employed. Rather, I listen very carefully to the emerging needs of the moment and then draw from a variety of approaches gathered over a period of almost 30 years.

Within the context of this essay, I can offer only limited examples. Although it is virtually impossible to communicate the actual experiences in words, hopefully the following will illustrate at least some dimension of the ideas here presented.

This is from the journal of a person with whom I worked over a concentrated period of time and is used here by permission from the participant:

> I focused on a dream I had…about my father. As I dropped more deeply into his gestureless gesture [in the dream], I noticed how strongly my attention was pulled to my/his left arm (the one which was broken and torn off by the oncoming car when I was 4 years old. And sewed back on and held together by metal pins for the rest of his life.) As I dreamed into his body, as I sank deeper and deeper, away from my mental body and into micro-sensations, I was aware that my left arm was completely cold! The rest of my body was warm.
>
> Re-emerging from this process, feeling my father in a visceral way, somehow opened the door of compassion [for him]. He was tormented by the death of my brother, his favorite son, and his love/disease of alcohol.
>
> I remember Cedrus' words: "When we drop deeply into our experience, physical, psychic and emotional defenses begin to crumble….Let the image drop from the mind into the body. That which listens, listens from the inside. Let the body become the ear in listening. If you feel like you're falling apart, that's perfect. If we stay intact, we'll never open up enough to be able to listen well."

As mentioned above, I also work with the embodiment of analysands' images that come from other than dreams. In this instance, we worked with a painting the analysand made when starting the analysis.

This particular painting was of a female torso standing on a surging sea of fang-like waves. Streaming out of the pelvic area was a large arc of dark red paint. She said she had no idea what the painting was about, but that she just "had to paint it." She was very concerned about the dark red area in the pelvic region.

I asked if she wanted to explore the painting through her own body, especially since it was an image of the body that she had painted. Although she expressed fear about what would come up, her desire to learn more took precedence. I asked if she would like to lie down on the floor; I put a pillow under her head and covered her with a blanket, letting her know that she could stop at any time. As she explored the image in her pelvic area by deeply connecting with that part of her body, that is, by moving her awareness down, listening, waiting for any impulses or sensations, she began to cry. She cried for a very long time, without saying anything. After she returned from this internal voyage, she said she realized the painting was about the abortion she had had years ago.

As a result of letting herself be guided by the body's impulses and sensations, prompted by the image from the unconscious in the form of her spontaneous painting, she was able to connect with her pain and grief. She was able to mourn the loss of her child and begin to release the oppressive shame and guilt that had engulfed her as a result. She had never told anyone before, holding the experience down, deep in her body for many years. Her long-held fear of never having a successful relationship or a child dissolved in the course of the analysis into a loving marriage and three beautiful children.

# Epilogue

It is my experience, as both patient and practitioner, that working through the body to access the unconscious is one of the most empowering venues for self-generative healing. Working through the body, we include aspects of life that have become dangerously marginalized. We begin to heal the wounding split that is created by the disenfranchisement of the very thing this approach embraces: the wisdom of the body, the somatic Sophia.

## REFERENCES

Chodorow, Joan (1991). *Dance Therapy and Depth Psychology: The Moving Imagination*. London: Routledge.

Jung, C. G. (1998). *Visions Seminar 2: Notes of the Seminar Given in 1930-1934*. London: Routledge; pp 1313-14.

Jung, C. G. (1954/1960). *On the Nature of the Psyche*. In CW 8.

Monte, Cedrus (2005). *Numen of the Flesh*. Quadrant XXXV,2: 11-31.

Rolf, Ida P. (1978/1990). *Rolfing and Physical Reality.* Rochester, Vermont: Healing Arts Press.

Woodman, Marion (1996). *Dancing in the Flames.* Boston: Shambala Press.

Corpus Anima

Fernando Pessoa , 1914

# In Consideration of Disquiet and Longing for Our Changing World

## Perspectives from the Poetry and Prose of Fernando Pessoa

This article first appeared in, *Analytical Psychology in a Changing World: The Search for Self, Identity and Community,* Ed. Lucy Huskinson and Murray Stein, Routledge, London and New York, 2014.

> I am the escaped one.
> After I was born
> They locked me up inside myself
>  But I left . . .
> My soul still seeks me
> Over hills and valley.
> I hope my soul
> Never finds me. (Pessoa 2006a, p. 315)

### Fernando Pessoa: a brief biography

Fernando Pessoa is considered Portugal's greatest contemporary writer. He was born Fernando António

Nogueira de Seabra Pessoa in Lisbon on June 13, 1888. He died on November 30, 1935, in the same city at the early age of forty-seven. Pessoa's mother, Maria Madalena Pinheiro Nogueira, originally from the Azores, was interested in both music and literature. His father, Joaquim de Seabra Pessoa, was a civil servant and a music critic for Lisbon's daily newspaper, *O Diário de Notícias*. On July 13, 1893, when Pessoa had just turned five, his father died of tuberculosis. The following year, on January 2, Pessoa's younger brother, Jorge, also died. He was only a year old. (Pessoa 2003)

Surrounded by death, Pessoa created his first literary companion, a pen pal by the name of Chevalier de Pas. Not only did Pessoa write to Chevalier de Pas, but his imaginary pen pal wrote back, acknowledging Pessoa's contact. These were the early beginnings of Pessoa's experience of the written word taking the form of reality, and the first of many characters to appear in his literary world. Through his writing, Pessoa began to create and re-create a world that would not only sustain him for the remainder of his life, but would create in literature a unique and completely original way of expressing and articulating the many dimensions of psyche.

In December of 1895, Pessoa's mother remarried João Miguel dos Santos Rosa, a military officer. The family moved to Durban, South Africa, where Pessoa's stepfather had been appointed the Portuguese consul. Pessoa attended the English-speaking schools there and continued to develop his desire for writing.

However, at the age of 17 after his early education in South Africa, Pessoa decided to come back to Lisbon and enrolled at the university. After his return, he rarely left the city.

Pessoa was a brilliant student, but due to difficult personal and political circumstances that ensued, he dropped out of the university not long after his seventeenth birthday and began to study on his own. He went to the National Library of Lisbon where he systematically read major works of philosophy, theology, history, sociology and, of course, literature, especially Portuguese literature. (Zenith 2008)

In 1916, one of Pessoa's closest friends and fellow poet, Mário de Sá-Carneiro, committed suicide. His friend's death affected him profoundly. It was at this point that Pessoa began to look for spiritual answers. To that end, he studied the cabala, alchemy, theosophy and other disciplines within the occult. He also became especially interested in astrology. Astrology was part of Pessoa's everyday life and he kept that interest until his death.

During his lifetime, Pessoa lived in rented rooms and later in a common residence with other members of his family. In 1920, Pessoa's mother returned to Lisbon from Durban after the death of her second husband. It was at this time that Pessoa rented living quarters for the reunited family—his mother, his half-sister and half-brothers and himself. The house is located in Lisbon on Rua Coelho da Rocha, 16. Today, this house is known as the *Casa Fernando Pessoa*. It houses a library, a bookstore, a museum, an art gallery and a lecture room, all open to the public. Admission is free. The world is fully and generously invited to participate in this extraordinary poet's life and work. Pessoa lived in this house for the last fifteen years of his life. (Zenith 2006)

From the website of *Casa Fernando Pessoa*, we find the following:

**A plural universe**

Opened in November 1993, the cultural centre Casa Fernando Pessoa was conceived by the Lisbon City Council as a tribute to Fernando Pessoa and his memory; it lies in the city where he lived and the area in which he spent the last fifteen years of his life, Campo de Ourique.

With its auditorium, garden, exhibition rooms, works of art, a library exclusively dedicated to poetry, in addition to part of the poet's estate (furniture and personal items that are now municipal heritage), the Casa Fernando Pessoa is a small but multifarious world. Its three floors host colloquia, poetry readings, meetings with authors, concerts and theatre, lectures, workshops, art exhibitions, book launches and children's ateliers in a programme of events which is as widely diversified as possible.

Pessoa was solitary by nature, having a limited social life and virtually no love life. He was, however, an active leader of Portugal's Modernist movement in the early 1900s. In Lisbon, he was respected as an intellectual and a poet yet, sadly, most of Pessoa's work was not published in his lifetime. He did publish his work in several magazines, some of which he helped to found, but his genius was essentially unrecognized by the world-at-large until after he died. (Zenith 2006)

At his death, his friends opened a large trunk in his apartment, discovering an estimated 25,000 pages of poems, essays, short stories and plays. Most of what we know of Pessoa's literary life comes from that trunk. More than ten decades after his death, Pessoa's vast body of writing has not yet been fully chronicled by researchers, and much of his prose is still to be published.

Pessoa was able to support himself financially as a commercial correspondent by writing letters in English and French for Portuguese companies that had business dealings abroad. Up until his death, he was largely employed as an independent commercial correspondent, working for individual companies on a contractual basis. He died without having acquired any material means beyond that which was needed for a simple existence.

## The soul of the poet

After his death, Pessoa became a national treasure. In 1988, 100 years after his birth, Pessoa was entombed at the Monastery of São Jeronimo in Lisbon, now a UNESCO World Heritage Site. Along with Luís Vaz de Camões, Portugal's much loved and celebrated 16th-century poet, Pessoa also presides here with Vasco de Gama, the fearless oceanic explorer from Portugal's Age of Discovery.

Pessoa was also a fearless explorer of inner worlds. The fact that this inner fearlessness is also recognized as greatness pays tribute not only to Pessoa, but to the culture and the people of Portugal who have honored this shy, eccentric and introverted artist.

An inscription on his tomb at São Jeronimo reflects the soul of Pessoa in four lines:

> I am nothing.
> I shall always be nothing.
> I cannot want to be anything.
> But I have in me all the dreams of the world
> (Alvaro do Campos; translation mine)

Since his death, Pessoa's reputation has grown throughout the world. He is recognized internationally as one of the major poets of the 20th century. To a certain audience within the general public, this modest and melancholy poet is something of a rock star, a cult figure who allows for the exploration of the deeper layers of the psyche, of life itself, life that is so often accompanied by quiet despair.

> I'm having one of those days when I feel I never had a future. There is only the present, fixed and encircled by a wall of anguish. The other bank of the river, because it is the other bank, is never the

bank we are standing on: and that is the intimate reason for all my suffering.

There are ships sailing to many different ports, but not a single one goes where life is not painful... All of this happened such a long time ago, but my sadness began even before then. (Pessoa 1998b, pp. 21–22, xxv)

Much of Pessoa's most famous work is attributed to four of his many heteronyms — Alberto Caeiro, Ricardo Reis, Álvaro de Campos and Bernardo Soares. The word "heteronym" was a term that Pessoa used rather than "pseudonym" (a name that one hides behind) in that each heteronym was, by design, an individual writer with a unique personality. Although it can be said that each writer reflects a dimension of Pessoa's multifaceted way of perceiving the world, as a heteronym each poet or writer speaks as a self-contained autonomous individual, unhindered or uncompromised by what might be interpreted as contradictions within the complex structure of Pessoa's nature and his vision of reality.

The apparent contradictions within Pessoa are, in fact, not contradictions. His need to express truth needed to come through the multiplicity of distinct voices. The invention of the many heteronyms allowed for each truth to unfold without the need to compromise or "relativize." Pessoa's heteronyms have their own separate personalities, their own biographies, individual signatures, and even their own astrological charts. They were each given their time to speak.

If we look at Pessoa's chart we learn that he was born with the sun in Gemini. He also has three other planets in Gemini, Gemini being the sign of the twins. For Pessoa, with four planets in the sign of twins, this quaternity of couplets creates much more than the sum of eight figures...it creates a virtual galaxy of heteronyms, over seventy in total, including one woman.

Pessoa could become whole only by giving voice to figure after figure within him. It was not only a matter of literary genius, it was also an act of following the soul: of living and expressing that constellation of energies that is intrinsically who we are, and is always calling us toward its fulfillment in and through our life experiences. Pessoa writes:

> I don't know how many souls I have...I've changed at every turn. I always feel like a stranger. I've never seen or found myself. From being so much, I am only soul...Attentive to what I am and to what I see, I become them. I stop being I. Each of my dreams and each desire belongs to whoever had it, not to me...(Pessoa 1998a)

Here again, from another perspective, he speaks of the multiplicity of being:

> I created myself, echo and abyss, by reflecting. I multiplied myself, by going deeply into myself. The smallest episode—a change of light, the crumpled fall of a dead leaf, the petal that drops off

and commits yellowcide, the voice on the far side of the wall...the half-open gate to the old estate, the patio that opens with an arch onto the houses heaped up in the moonlight – all these things, which do not belong to me, tie up my sensory reflections with chords of resonance and nostalgia. In each one of these sensations I am someone else, I renew myself painfully in each indefinite impression.

I live on impressions that don't belong to me, reckless with renunciations, just another version of myself.(Pessoa 1998b, pp. 21–22)

Continuing with Pessoa's astrological portrait, one finds that he also had a strong emphasis in what is known as the eighth house of the astrological chart. (Each chart is divided into twelve houses or aspects of life, corresponding with the twelve signs of the zodiac.) In large part, the eighth house represents the dimension of the psyche that is involved with death and rebirth, with deep transformational forces that regulate and demand the repeated release of established forms and structure, allowing for continual rebirth. The mythical phoenix is an appropriate image of this process.

The eighth house also delineates the area of the psyche that is most related to depth analytical psychology: transformation through the death of the lesser ego through the constant integration of the unconscious and its vivifying effects. Apropos to this particular expression of transformation, when speaking of the integration of the unconscious in relation to the ego, Jung says: "The secret is that only that which can destroy itself is truly alive." (Jung 1968, par. 93) Jung was suggesting that for every insight that arises from the unconscious and integrated into conscious life, that integration is experienced as a death by the ego—that is, the ego must relinquish its more limited and confined vision to a wisdom that is greater than itself.

It is only by accepting the death of what is no longer viable that we can be truly alive. From the piece of the cosmos that Pessoa was given to explore, astrologically speaking, one can say that Pessoa had been given an open account with the unconscious (also an eighth house concern), forever venturing into and integrating new territory through character after character, heteronym after heteronym. In this, Pessoa was a companion with his fellow compatriots, those mariners and navigators who for centuries crossed what was indeed the great unknown in their numerous *caravelas*, swift and highly nimble ships, carrying them across uncharted waters, making the unknown, "unconscious" world known.

To venture into the outer unknown, we need to confront our physical death. To venture into the inner unknown, the ego must die to the deeper wisdom of the unconscious, again and again. It was this inner venture that Pessoa helped to chart for us through his vision and through his literary opus.

Thus, from his astrological destiny, as well as for other root reasons, Pessoa had a natural inclination toward the impulses in life that request our acceptance of death as the fundamental road toward a fuller life. He lived with this paradox intimately every day, from early childhood until his physical death, as the core and essence of his life and work as an artist. This natural inclination would be no small factor in Pessoa's influence as one of the greatest contemporary writers of Portugal, and beyond. He speaks and writes of the taboos held within the underbelly of life and death. In his psychological sensitivity and literary skill he allows us to claim our own fears and unlived life forces, helping us to confront our uncertainties about death.

## The Book of Disquiet

> To understand I had to destroy myself. To understand is to forget about loving. (Pessoa 2006b, section 48)

This quotation appears in what is perhaps Pessoa's greatest sustained individual work, *The Book of Disquiet*, penned by Bernardo Soares. Soares is the heteronym that was most like Pessoa himself. He was a quiet clerk in Lisbon, an accountant working in an office. This is a world that Pessoa knew quite well due to his long career as a correspondence translator.

*The Book*, as it is also known, was first published forty-seven years after Pessoa's death. Now published in thirty-seven languages, *The Book* is a bestseller, especially in German, with sixteen editions. The *Book of Disquiet* is a haunting mosaic of dreams, psychological reflections and autobiographical vignettes. Listed as one of the top 100 books of all time, Pessoa's *Book of Disquiet* was discovered in the trunk in his apartment after his death.

In a period of over two decades, Pessoa recorded his reveries and impressions. It is an exploration of paradox, an expression of his astute and penetrating melancholy.

> In its essence all life is monotonous. Happiness therefore depends on a reasonably thorough adaptation to life's monotony. By making ourselves monotonous, we make ourselves the same as life. We thus live to the full. And living to the full is to be happy.

> I always acted on the inside...I was never able to touch life... I enjoyed strolling alone through green parks and down wide corridors...In the broad and dusky corridor at the back of the palace, I often strolled with my fiancée...though I never had a real fiancée...I never knew how to love... I only knew how to dream of loving...If I liked to wear ladies' rings on my fingers, it's because I sometimes supposed that my hands belonged to a princess and that I, at least in the movements of my hands, was the woman I loved...It isn't me who's telling you this...Who's speaking is what's left of me. (Pessoa 2006b, section 342)

> I turned myself into a fiction of myself to such a degree that any natural feeling I have, of course, from the moment it's born, becomes a feeling of the

imagination — the memory in dreams, the dream of forgetting about the dream, knowing myself by not reflecting on myself.

I stripped off my own being to such an extent that existing means dressing up. Only when I'm disguised am I truly myself. And around me all unknown sunsets as they die, make golden the landscapes I shall never see. (Pessoa 1998b, p. 55)

## Disquiet and longing for our changing world

So how does this shy, introverted man become one of Portugal's greatest artists? How does he become a rock star of the soul in the world-at-large? I would suggest it is because humanity desperately longs for what Pessoa gives voice to. It longs to feel what we have largely rejected in the pursuit of what we think is perfect happiness and worldly success. We long to feel the disquiet and despair that we lock away in our closet of skeletons. We long for the release of our tightly withheld lament. And, I would suggest, humanity longs to understand the deeper meaning of longing, which mystical traditions recognize as the homesickness of the soul yearning for its true Home.

The Sufi mystics understood this longing as the core of the spiritual quest (and mystic Islam would not be foreign to the Portuguese psyche, with the Moors having ruled in the Iberian Peninsula from approximately AD700 to AD1200).

Llewellyn Vaughan-Lee, Sufi mystic and lineage successor in the Naqshbandiyya-Mujaddidiyya Sufi Order, writes:

> Longing is the central core of every mystical path, as the anonymous author of the fourteenth-century mystical classic, The Cloud of Unknowing, simply states: 'Your whole life must be one of longing.' Yet our present Western society is so divorced from this mystical thread that underlies every spiritual path that we have no context within which to appreciate the nature of the heart's desire for Truth. There are many people who feel the unhappiness of a homesick soul and yet do not know its cause. They do not realize the wonder of their pain, that it is their heart's longing that will take them Home. (Vaughan-Lee Summer 1999)

Longing and lament, disquiet and despair are largely marginalized in the greater collective and often seen as pathological in the more extroverted, success-driven world. A place and time to lament what has been lost, space to experience our longing for that which is beyond temporal fulfillment, finds little place or recognition. Pessoa's quest compels us to ask what we can redeem in psychic wholeness by making a place for these abandoned soul forces.

Pessoa did not turn away from his sense of desolation. Paradoxically, fragilely, even at great cost to his own physical being, he discovered and recreated himself within it. Perhaps it is this fragile, yet fierce and fearless search that the Portuguese, and in fact the world-at-large, have understood as greatness.

Pessoa was talented, yes, but his genius goes beyond literary talent. In his experience of marginalization, he created a meaningful center, no matter its vulnerability. Through his writing he created a center for himself, for himself and for others who feel a sense of longing and disquiet that can never be fully eased. Pessoa's life was in constant tension with no apparent resolution. He was often tormented. But that he searched and endured and wrote as he did was itself the resolution.

"Everything I wanted in life, I abandoned for the sake of the search." (Pessoa 2006b, section 342) Pessoa's life-long search for meaning, stemming from a continual sense of disquiet and despair, from an ever-present experience of longing and lament, gives us a template from which to better understand the redemptive nature of disquiet and longing for our changing world.

We cannot give into despair, yet we cannot move forward without acknowledging it. To continuously re-create our world, to survive, we must learn how to live within the tensions of paradox: peace is the partner of disquiet; to learn about wholeness, we must invite that for which we long; without time for lament, our happiness becomes frenetic, empty.

In Pessoa's writing, we find clues to holding the tension of opposing energies and to finding meaning in the haunting sense of meaninglessness that can spur the disconsolate soul forward into the search, toward the journey Home.

Pessoa also writes from a sense of hopelessness that is just as paradoxical as the sense of despair and longing that he communicates:

> In those slow empty hours there arises from my soul to my mind a sadness that encompasses my entire being, the bitterness of all being...which is not within my power to change...The peace of anguish is in my heart, and my serenity is made of resignation. (Pessoa 1998b, p.45)

Although Pessoa did not live in the same time historically as Tibetan Buddhist nun and teacher, Pema Chödron, they would have no doubt understood each other. To understand the sense of hopelessness and uncertainty from a spiritual perspective, Chödron offers her teachings. She says, "If we're willing to give up hope that insecurity and pain can be exterminated, then we can have the courage to relax with the groundlessness of our situation." (Chödron 1997, p. 38)

She continues further by explaining:

> Turning our mind toward spiritual teachings does not bring security or confirmation of hope. It does not bring any ground to stand on. In fact, when one's mind turns toward spiritual teachings, one begins to fearlessly acknowledge impermanence and we begin to get the knack of hopelessness. (ibid.)

We begin to acknowledge that we cannot hide from a life that includes chaos, death and uncertainty. While Chodrön is not suggesting that life is hopeless, she does offer that if we do not include chaos, death and impermanence in our lives we will be denying the intrinsic nature of life itself.

Chödron continues:

> In the process of discovering bodhichitta [an awakened heart], the journey goes down, not up. It's as if the mountain pointed toward the center of the earth instead of reaching into the sky. Instead of transcending the suffering of all creatures, we move toward the turbulence and doubt. We jump into it. We slide into it. We tiptoe into it. We move toward it however we can. We explore the reality and unpredictability of insecurity and pain, and we try not to push it away. If it takes years, if it takes lifetimes, we let it be as it is...Right down there in the thick of things, we discover the love that will not die. (Chödron 1997, p. 39)

This was also Pessoa's search and struggle, to understand this perspective in his own way in his own time and in his own system of belief, and in particular through his explorations in the *Book of Disquiet*. He may not have experienced these paradoxical truths as fully integrated into his personal life—he most likely would not have chosen to go down this path of engaging the darker areas of longing and despair of his own accord —but it is apparently certain that Pessoa's *daimon* had set sights on the exploration of this shadowy territory. Thus, with the trembling of hopelessness coupled with a persistent lack of fear, Pessoa ventured into the uncertainty of these unknown forces as a navigator of the depths, showing the way for those willing to follow.

In addition to his ventures in the *Book of Disquiet*, Pessoa's search continues in the only book he published in Portuguese, *Mensagem*, or *Message*.

# Pessoa's Message and the Age of the Holy Spirit

*Message*

It is not only the redemptive powers of disquiet, longing and uncertainty that Pessoa called forth within the hearts of others. He also sent us a message of another kind. Published just one year before his death, *Mensagem*, or *Message*, is a three-part, multi-layered complexity of forty-four short poems, a symbolist epic interconnecting nation with the individual self, calling the reader forward to a spiritual quest.

The first section of *Mensagem*, entitled *Brasão*, or *Coat-of-Arms*, speaks of both the material and spiritual dimensions of Portugal, all leading to the Golden Age of Discovery that started in the early 15th century and continued up to the 17th century.

The second section of the epic is entitled *Mar Português*, or *Portuguese Sea*. It starts with the time of the

Discoveries and the empire that was built through Portuguese oceanic exploration, and ends with the demise of Portugal's young king, Sebastião, or Sebastian (January 20, 1554 – August 4, 1578). One of the most famous of Pessoa's poems is in this second section and has the same name, *Mar Português*. It describes the perils of these oceanic adventures into the unknown as well as the costs for global expansion. As such, one may understand that Pessoa was speaking not only of the outer journey but also, symbolically, of the inward voyage one must undertake for an expanded experience of consciousness.

> Portuguese Sea
> Salt-filled sea, how much of your salt
> Is tears of Portugal!
> For us to cross you, how many mothers wept
> How many sons kept Vigil in vain!
> Lived as old maids how many brides-to-be
> Till death, so that you might be ours, sea!
> Was it all worth while? It is worth while, all,
> If the soul is not small.
> Whoever intends to sail beyond the Cape
> Must double sorrow – no escape.
> God to the sea has given peril and abyss
> But has yet made it the mirror of heaven.
> (Pessoa 2007, p. 73)

Finally, part three of *Mensagem*, *O Encoberto*, or *The Hidden One*, refers to the return of the lost king (in this case, King Sebastian). *The Hidden One* speaks of the fulfillment of humanity's destiny, which is predestined or designed by God, and of Portugal's implied role in this destiny. The return of the lost king, Sebastian, follows the archetypal "return of the king" (such as found in the legend of King Arthur) whereupon the king returns in the darkest hour to help his people. For the Portuguese, *The Hidden One* would return on a foggy morning to save Portugal.

In *Message*, the historical human figures from Portugal's past are symbols for the spiritual quest, and the ordeals of the ocean mariners describe the need for individual resolve and perseverance. The quest is to reconnect not only the individual but also Portugal back to historical, mystical roots. As such, Pessoa interjects an underlying current in the poem that refers to the prophetic tradition of the Age of the Holy Spirit, wherein a new epoch of peace and concord begins. This era would coincide with the return of the lost king.

### The Age of the Holy Spirit

Portugal's history is particularly connected to the Age of the Holy Spirit. Before describing that history and its deeper meaning, however, a brief explanation of the Holy Spirit and the Age of the Holy Spirit will serve as an introduction.

Theologically, the Holy Spirit, often represented as a white dove, is the third person of the Christian Trinity with God the Father and God the Son. This third is known equally as the Holy Spirit, the Holy Ghost, or the Paraclete (meaning "comforter" in Greek). In the Old Testament, the Holy Spirit is shown as the life-giving breath of God. In the New Testament, Christians believe that the Holy Spirit is God working in the world, the *activity* of God on earth. Contemporary theologians, Shults and Hollingsworth, describe the Holy Spirit "as both the divine ground of all life...as well as the presence that engenders experiences of transformed life," for example, healing and prophetic insight. (Shults and Hollingsworth 2008, pp. 2, 3)

Historically, the medieval theologian, Joachim de Fiore (*c*.1135 to March 30, 1202), wrote about The Age of the Holy Spirit as an age in which the necessity for texts, church structures and organizations would be overcome and be drawn into the living spirit, living not by texts or hierarchical authorities. Organizations would be left behind and people would be able to tune into spiritual life on their own. Joachim de Fiore was the founder of the monastic order of San Giovanni in Fiore (in Italy). He was a mystic and a theologian, born in a small village in Calabria, at that time part of the Kingdom of Sicily.

> He theorized the dawn of a new age in which the hierarchy of the church would be unnecessary. Members of the *spiritual* wing of the *Franciscan* order acclaimed him as a prophet. Though theoretically controversial according to some, the holiness of his life was widely known: *Dante* affirmed that miracles were said to have taken place at his tomb and, though never officially beatified, he is still venerated on May 29. (Wikipedia: website)

The mystical basis of Fiore's Theory of the Three Ages is founded on his interpretation of the biblical text, The Book of Revelation. He believed that history, by analogy with the Trinity, was divided into three fundamental epochs: The Age of the Father, corresponding to the Old Testament and the obedience of humanity to the letter of the law; The Age of the Son, when Man becomes the son of God; and the Age of the Holy Spirit wherein humanity has a direct relationship with God and has the full understanding and experience of universal love. Fiore believed that only in the Age of the Holy Spirit would it be possible to understand the writings of God in their deepest meaning, not just in the literal sense. And, rather than the Second Coming of Christ, an era of peace and harmony would reign, making the hierarchy of the Church unnecessary.

Unfortunately, it would seem, Fiore was a man far ahead of his time. He saw this all coming to pass in the 13th century. He concluded that this age would begin in 1260 based on the Book of Revelation, verses 11:3 and 12:6, which mention "one thousand two hundred and sixty days." (Wikipedia: website)

Not incongruent with Fiore's theory, Jung saw the Age of the Holy Spirit as a time when the individual would live spiritual life independent of sacred texts or dogma. He saw it as a time when we would be able to experience the numinous in direct communion, not through the hierarchy of religious authority.

During a seminar with Murray Stein, Jungian analyst, Stein was asked what Jung meant when he said, "Things will be resolved in the age of the Holy Spirit." Stein's response (paraphrased) was that Jung understood that the psyche works through polarities that require us to hold tension or conflict, out of which comes the third, resolved thing. In the development of the doctrine of the Trinity, the third—the Holy Spirit— comes out of the two, the Father and the Son and the third unites the two. The development of the doctrine of the Trinity is this dialectic that leads to a third. The Age of the Holy Spirit is not a collapse of the difference between one polarity and the other, but the resolution of the polarities by holding them in a container that is big enough to lift both opposites into wholeness... this would be considered the Age of the Holy Spirit.

Stein also noted that the Age of the Holy Spirit is an age in which necessity for texts are overcome; people are drawn into life through the living spirit, not through Church authorities. Jung, Stein said, saw this as an essential need in the psyche, and that individuals are capable of accessing spiritual life on their own through dreams and active imagination—for example, independent of sacred texts.

Stein continues by saying that Jung encouraged the making of one's own sacred text out of personal material, not handed down by outer authority (*The Red Book* being the primary example of this). He saw the spiritual future as an age of the individual, of freedom, where the need for Church and doctrines would be left behind, tuning into a spiritual life where we are capable of experiencing the numinous individually, not through external authorities. Jung saw this as the future for religion on this planet, just as the medieval theologian Joachim de Fiore did centuries before. (Asheville Jung Center: website)

As mentioned above, Portugal is especially attuned to the Age of the Holy Spirit as a result of its own mystical, historical roots. It is a subject too complex to fully cover within the limitations of this chapter, but a brief description will help reveal the depth of the *Message* that Pessoa leaves with us.

The members of the Knights Templar built many castles, churches and towns in Portugal. In 1307, King Philip IV of France, in debt with the Order, arrested and burned the Knights Templar at the stake. In 1312 Pope Clement V disbanded this powerful and rich order. After the extinction of the Order in 1312, King Dinis of Portugal (1261–1325) renamed the Portuguese branch, calling it the Order of Christ and left it to go about its business as usual. Prince Henry the Navigator (1394–1460), mastermind of the 16th-century discoveries, was himself a leader of this Order. The ships that sailed from Portugal carried the flag of the cross of the Order of Christ. These facts and developments are the foundation of a vast literature of mystic nationalism that speculates on the real aim of the Portuguese discoveries. (Santos and Farias 2002)

In the early 1300s, during the same period that King Dinis created the Order of Christ, Joachim de Fiore's Theory of the Three Ages began to spread throughout

Portugal. Cistercian and Franciscan monks were the first to take the theory seriously, but the royal family, King Dinis and his Queen, Isabel, were also moved. As we read above, Fiore's vision proclaimed the imminent rise of an Age of the Holy Spirit. In this new age, humanity would receive a gospel by direct dispensation from the Holy Spirit and the ideal of universal brotherhood would finally become a reality. (Santos and Farias 2002)

The celebrations and festivities of the Holy Spirit, or the Holy Ghost, began during the reign of King Dinis and Queen Isabel (1270–1336) at about 1305. The widespread popular adherence that quickly followed spread the celebrations throughout the mainland and subsequently to the overseas possessions, constituting a phenomenon unparalleled in other Christian countries. The main features of these festivities were, and largely still are, the coronation of a child or man, usually of low social standing, symbolizing that the Empire of the Spirit belongs to the simple and innocent ones — those without cunning or guile or worldliness; a ritualized, collective banquet for hundreds of people in each village or locale, symbolizing generosity for the common good, supporting brotherhood and sisterhood among all people; and (then, but not now) the unchaining of certain (non-violent) prisoners, symbolizing the liberation of humankind.

Prohibitions by the Catholic Church contributed to the progressive deterioration of these festivities on the Portuguese mainland, but they are still very much alive in the Atlantic Azorean Archipelago, and in many

Azorean emigrant communities in the USA and Canada.

The festival of the Holy Ghost is a unique Portuguese feast for those of Portuguese-speaking countries or communities to experience as a Pentecostal act. Although the festival takes place over many weeks, the main events take place on Pentecost Sunday, the day the Paraclete, the Holy Spirit, came down in flames over the heads of the apostles inspiring them to go out and bring the teachings and prophesies of God into the world.

The Age of the Holy Spirit would re-emerge as a concept throughout the history of Portuguese mystical thought. (Santos and Farias 2002)

In their book *The Holy Spirit,* Shults and Hollingsworth give the following examples of what the Holy Spirit was and is considered to be in Christian theology. The italics are mine, calling the reader's attention to those ideas that relate directly to the Age of the Holy Spirit prophesied by Fiore, and which the Portuguese festivals are intended to commemorate. They also call attention to the archetypal elements included in the mystical, historical roots of Portugal, its culture and its people:

> Paul connects the experience of the Holy Spirit to the flourishing of the community in his letter to the Romans. God's love "has been poured into our hearts through the Holy Spirit." (Prov 5:5) *The Spirit is the source of the community's love, freedom,*

*and hope for renewal.* (Shults and Hollingsworth 2008, pp. 4, 5)

One of Paul's central themes is the way in which the Holy Spirit creates, upholds, and enlivens the community of believers. *The "gifts" of the Spirit, which are manifested through individual voices, are primarily intended for communal contexts and for the common good of everyone.* (Cor 1:12) (Shults and Hollingsworth 2008, pp. 4, 5)

Those who are led by the Spirit are not subject to [the letter of the] law, but *Spirit-filled living results in loving, patient,* gentle *attitudes and actions toward others.* (Gal 5:18–23) (Shults and Hollingsworth 2008, pp. 4, 5)

The Holy Spirit not only anoints bodies and enlivens voices, but also *calls them outward toward serving others, into the world to do the work of the divine kingdom of peace and justice.* (Shults and Hollingsworth 2008, pp. 4, 5)

Returning now to Pessoa's poetic epic, *Message* is a call to the soul, the individual soul and the soul of a nation. It is a call to fulfill a certain destiny: the embodiment of a mystical consciousness that engenders profound experiences of transformed life in service to the common good, a consciousness that is embedded in the greater collective soul of a nation and of humanity as a whole. It is a call to enter into the essence of the Age of the Holy Spirit, the dimension of life that embodies the mystical nature of the psyche.

In the last poem of *Message*, Pessoa refers to Portugal as Portugal itself, and also, perhaps, as yet another heteronym, as another figure within him, and also, perhaps, within us:

### Fog

Neither king nor law, neither peace nor war
Can define the outline and the truth
Of, look!, that radiant gleam of the earth
That's Portugal, breaking the heart –
A flaring without light or heat,
Like the core of an ethereal flame.
No one knows what she desires.
No one understands what soul is hers,
Not what is bad, nor what is good,
(What distant agony mourning near?)
All's uncertain and is at the end,
All is scattered, nothing entire.
O Portugal, fog you are . . . and yet
Comes the Hour! (Pessoa 2007, p. 107)

## Epilogue

Comes the hour...from out of a foggy morning comes the 'lost king,' *The Hidden One*, a hidden consciousness now coming to light, returning to redeem what has been lost, what we have lost. To remind us that a new Empire of the Spirit, a Holy Spirit, is to be built from a consciousness that can embrace the complexity of paradoxical truths and lead us out of the polarization of fundamentalism and hatred. To remind us that a world can be built from a consciousness crafted for and in service to the common good, a consciousness that can hold the tensions of life's natural polarities and lift them into wholeness.

It is indeed the hour in our critically changing world not to marginalize the more difficult dimensions of a life fully lived. It is the hour to embrace both joy *and* despair, to accept both peace *and* disquiet, to rejoice *and* to openly lament. Most importantly, it is the hour to embrace our greater destiny, the mystical Oneness that forever holds and re-creates our scattered, uncertain and fragmented lives.

Fernando Pessoa, the one in whom *all the dreams of the world* exist, helps guide us to this embrace.

**NOTE**

Although the translations of Pessoa's poems are my own, for ease of reference for the reader, I cite the passages as they appear in the familiar translations by Richard Zenith, published by Grove (1998) and Penguin (2006), and by Jonathan Griffin, published by Shearsman.

**REFERENCES**

Asheville Jung Center (website). 'The Age of the Holy Spirit: Transcending the polarities of God the Father and God the Son,' seminar. Online. Available: http://ashevillejungcenter.org/2010/06/age-of-holy-spirit-transcending-polarities-of-god-father-god-son/ (accessed 24 May 2011).

Casa Fernando Pessoa (website). Online. Available: http://casafernandopessoa.cm- lisboa.pt/index.php? id=2258&L=4 (accessed 22 September 2012).

Chödron, P. (1997) When Things Fall Apart: Heart Advice for Difficult Times, Boston, MA and London: Shamballa.

Jung, C.G. (1968) *Psychology and Alchemy. Volume 12. The Collected Works of C. G. Jung*, trans. R.F.C. Hull, Bollingen Series XX, Princeton, NJ: Princeton University Press.

Pessoa, F. (2003) *Escritos Autobiográficos, Automáticos e de Reflexão Pessoal*, Assírio and Alvim, 'Chronology established by R. Zenith and corrected by him for inclusion on our site. Sources for the information can be found in the cited edition.' Online. Available: http://casafernandopessoa.cm-lisboa.pt/index.php? id=4285&L=4 (accessed 15 September 2012).

Pessoa, F. (1998) *Fernando Pessoa & Co. – Selected Poems*, trans. R. Zenith, New York: Grove Press. Online. Available: www.poetryinternationalweb.net/pi/site/ poem/item/7084 (accessed 9 September 2012).

Pessoa, F. (1998b) *The Book of Disquiet*, composed by Bernardo Soares, Assistant Bookkeeper in the City of Lisbon, trans. Alfred Mac Adam, Boston, MA: Exact Change.

Pessoa, F. (2006) A Little Larger than the Entire Universe: Selected Poems, trans. R. Zenith, New York and London: Penguin.

Pessoa, F. (2006b) *The Book of Disquiet*, 'A Factless Autobiography,' Richard Zenith Edition, Lisbon.

Pessoa, F. (2007) *Message/Mensagem*, trans. Jonathan Griffin, Exeter and London: Shearsman Books and The Menard Press.

Santos, T. and Farias, M (2002) 'Religion in Portugal,' in Dr. J. Gorden Melton (ed.) *The 21st Century Encyclopedia of World Religion,* Santa Barbara, USA: 2002. Online. Available: www.prolades.com/cra/regions/ibero/port-eng/Portugal,%20 Religion%20in.htm (accessed 5 September 2012).

Shults, F. and Hollingsworth, A. (2008) *The Holy Spirit,* Grand Rapids, MI/Cambridge, UK: William B. Eerdmans Publishing Company.

Vaughan-Lee, L. (Summer 1999) 'Love and Longing: The Feminine Mysteries of Love.' *Personal Transformation*. Online. Available: http://goldensufi.org/a_love_ and_longing.html> (accessed 15 September 2012).

Wikipedia (website). Online. Available: http://en.wikipedia.org/wiki/Joachim_of_ Fiore> (accessed 14 September 2012).

Zenith, R. (2006) *The 'Real' Fernando Pessoa: a biographical sketch*. Online. Available: www.poetryinternationalweb.net/pi/site/cou_article/item/7098/The-Real-Fernando-Pessoa-a-biographical-sketch> (accessed 22 September 2012).

Zenith, R. (2006) *The 'Real' Fernando Pessoa: a biographical sketch*. Online. Available: www.poetryinternationalweb.net/pi/site/cou_article/item/7098/The-Real-Fernando-Pessoa-a-biographical-sketch (accessed 22 June 2012).

Zenith, R. (2008) *Fernando Pessoa (Fotobiografias Século XX)*, Lisboa: Círculo de Leitores. Online. Available: http://en.wikipedia.org/wiki/Fernando_Pessoa (accessed 20 September 2012).

Corpus Anima

# The Azores and the Secrets of the Land

The following articles were written for two on-line newspapers located in São Miguel, Azores: Mundo Açoreano and Jornal Diário. The Azores are an archipelago of nine islands about 900 miles off the coast of Portugal at the confluence of three tectonic plates, otherwise known as the Azores Triple Junction. Some say these islands, the tops of the highest mountain range in the world, the Mid-Atlantic Ridge, are part of what was once Atlantis.

The Azores have a 600 year old tradition of celebrating the Holy Spirit. The celebrations are non-hierarchical in structure, organized not by the church but by the people, perhaps holding the prophesied Age of the Holy Spirit *in utero* where there is no religious dogma, rather peace and equality for all and a direct communion with the divine. The following articles propose that the soul of the land conjoins with the soul of the people to hold and maintain this extraordinary vision.

São Miguel is where my soul came to incarnate into this world.

# 1. Secrets of the Land

The Swiss psychiatrist (and mystic) C. G. Jung, once wrote, "Every soil has its secret of which we carry an unconscious image in our souls." Every soil, every land, lives and expresses its secret through us, through the lives of the people that live upon the land. At the root of this idea is the universal understanding in mystical traditions that spirit and matter are not separate. They are reflections of each other. They are one.

To take this idea further, I would like your help in speculating on this question:

*What is the secret of the Azorean soil that lives and expresses itself as the Azorean people, as the Azorean soul?*

For me, this is not merely a hypothetical question. As one who has roots in the Azores, it is a deeply personal question. The quest to understand what energies lie at the depths of my own psyche in relation to my ancestors and the land of my ancestors has been lifelong.

Before any possible answer to the question can be formulated, it is important to know at least something of the nature of the soil, the nature of the Azorean land itself. I start with this example, only one of many possibilities:

In the Atlantic Ocean, the Azores rest about 900 miles off the coast of Portugal, at the center-point of where three tectonic plates intersect: the North American Plate, the Eurasian Plate and the African Plate. This triple junction is located along the Mid-Atlantic Ridge (part of the highest mountain range in the world). Along the tectonic plates, deep-sea hydrothermal vents form as a result of the shifting and moving of the earth's plates.

As I've written elsewhere in a professional journal, *Quadrant*:

"Deep-sea hydrothermal vents arise through volcanic activity at the meeting place of the Continental Plates where the earth's crust is formed. Hydrothermal vents are one of the most toxic environments on the planet, emitting lethal concentrations of hydrogen sulfites. Here, in the lethal environment of the vents, scientists have discovered extraordinary sites of what some consider to be bio-genesis: the spontaneous emergence of new life. At a depth of 8,600 feet, new species of subterranean flora and fauna spontaneously arise in prolific numbers and thrive in the toxic environment through the process of chemosynthesis."

In the situation described above, new life (bio-genesis) appears alongside eruption, lethal toxicity, trauma and destruction. Hydrothermal vents may offer us, then, in geophysical form, vital clues for undertaking what I consider to be one of the greatest spiritual tasks of our time. The vents show us that it is possible for life to thrive in spite of, and even more importantly, because of, events we typically believe to be destructive to life. Life not only thrives in these zones of trauma and eruption, but new life forms arise. Here at these sites there is a continual, paradoxical pattern of the destruction of what currently exists, yet with the result of new and greater life being formed.

Taking this a step further: At the physical level, the vents might reflect to us that at the spiritual level the sacrifice of individual needs can bring us into connection with new life, and in service to the common good. (Is this not, in part, what the Festival of the Holy Spirit in the Azores celebrates?)

What some are calling bio-genesis, then, may be the counterpart to what can be called psycho-genesis. From my perspective, psycho-genesis is a profound renewal of life through the necessary, organic and regenerative forces of death. It was this understanding that the ancient Greeks practiced through the Eleusinian Mysteries, for example, and perhaps elsewhere...perhaps even in Atlantis.

*So how might the soul of the Azorean people be influenced by these particular energies of the land where death and bio-genesis are an everyday part of life (even if it is largely unconscious and deeply subterranean)? And how might life move and manifest uniquely through the Azorean people as a result of these energies?*

Do these energies help the people generate new life out of destruction, to live and thrive in spite of, or because of, the extremes found in this location?

Given that matter and spirit are not separate, I think there is a connection. But that is only my opinion.

What is yours?

# 2. The Presence of the Paraclete

Last week I proposed a question for us to reflect upon:

*How might the soul of the Azorean people be influenced by these particular energies of the land...? And how might life move and manifest uniquely through the Azorean people as a result...?*

One possible answer might come from considering the Festival of the Holy Spirt, its roots, intentions and practices.

Historically, the celebration of the Holy Spirit and its traditions involve Joachim de Fiore, mystic, theologian, and founder of the monastic order of San Giovanni in Fiore (Italy) (circa 1135 to March 30, 1202). Fiore theorized an Age of the Holy Spirit in which humanity would receive the gospel directly from the Holy Spirit, where the ideal of universal fellowship would finally become a reality. In this age, the necessity for texts, hierarchical church structures and organizations would be overcome.

The mystical basis of Fiore's Theory of the Three Ages is founded on his interpretation of the biblical text, The Book of Revelation. He believed that history was divided into three fundamental epochs: The Age of the Father, corresponding to the Old Testament; The Age of the Son, based on the redemption of humanity through Christ; and the Age of the Holy Spirit, where humankind has a direct relationship with God as well as the full understanding and experience of universal love. An era of peace and harmony would reign in this epoch, making the hierarchy of the Church unnecessary.

Fiore's ideas began to spread throughout Portugal. Cistercian and Franciscan monks were the first to take the theory seriously; but the Portuguese royal family, King Dinis and Queen Isabel, were also moved. The celebrations of the Holy Spirit began during their reign in about 1305. They quickly spread throughout the mainland and to overseas possessions, constituting a phenomenon unparalleled in other Christian countries.

The main features of these festivities were the coronation of a child or man, necessarily of humble social standing, symbolizing that The Empire of the Spirit belongs to the simple and innocent; a ritualized, collective banquet given to often hundreds of people in each village, symbolizing generosity for the common good, supporting fellowship among all people; and the freeing of certain (non-violent) prisoners, symbolizing the liberation of humankind. Prohibitions by the Catholic Church contributed to the deterioration of these festivities on the Portuguese mainland, but they are still very much alive in the Azores.

*Why have these practices remained intact in the Azores and largely untouched?*

I propose, as suggested in the previous post, it might lie in the "secret of the soil," a secret that is whispered to the soul of the Azorean people. I propose that the geophysical soul lives in the traditions and practices of the Azorean people in this way. Allow me to explain further:

The people of the Azores live in constant awareness of existential uncertainty through the earth's shifting and shaking and volcanic eruptions. They live at the center of three tectonic plates and their unpredictable seismic activity. There is probably no greater invitation than these conditions to recognize that our existence depends upon the connection not only to physical ground, but also to spiritual ground. With this level of radical uncertainty, it would only be prudent, if not inspired, to realize that life, all life, would be furthered by a devotion that includes living from a heartfelt connection to the divine, direct and unmediated, and in consideration of the common good.

As we have read, this is how the Age of the Holy Spirit has been described. And so, too, the traditions and practices of the cult of the Holy Spirit as practiced in the Azores.

For 600 years the people of the Azores have been devoted to encouraging the living presence of the Paraclete, the Holy Spirit—advocate, intercessor, protector, comforter, the presence of the divine at work in the world—in the annual celebrations of the Holy Spirit. Can we say that the soul of the land has claimed the people for this destiny? Can we say that the soil shares its secrets with them in this way, for the greater and common good? I think we can.

To be continued.

# 3. DEEPER MYSTICAL ROOTS

Some of the following ideas may challenge our conventional understanding, so an open mind is needed.

The mystical roots of the Holy Spirit seem to go deeper than Fiore's theory. (Please refer to last post.) They lead us to a time not long after the death of Jesus when the Holy Spirit was not considered masculine, but feminine.

When ancient Christian texts dated from the first two centuries A.D. were found in Egypt (1945) and near Jerusalem (1947), no one had known that some groups of early Christians had an image of the Divine Mother whom they had named "The Invisible Within All."

It may also be an even greater surprise to learn that they understood this Divine Mother as the Holy Spirit and saw the dove as her emissary.

From contemporary scholars (e.g., Elaine Pagels) we learn that every secret text which early Christian groups revered was omitted and considered heretical by those who called themselves orthodox Christians. In so omitting these texts, all feminine references for God disappeared. For example, in one of the manuscripts the prayers invoke the Holy Spirit as "the Mother of All Creation."

These early Christians saw the Divine Mother as the womb of life, not only of human life, but that of the whole cosmos. The Divine Mother, the Holy Spirit, was considered the energy that pervades and sustains all.

What might this mean in relation to the experience and celebration of the Holy Spirit and in relation to the secret of the land as we have discussed it in the last two posts?

If we agree, if only for the sake of our present discussion, with the view of early Christians who knew the Holy Spirit as the Mother of All Creation (the energy that is "the invisible within all") — land, tree, bird, stone, fellow human — we can better understand the earth as a living, co-creative being. We can better understand that the soil of the land is alive and in direct kinship with the life and soul of the people.

If we understand, if only for the present moment, the possibility of the Holy Spirit as deeply interrelated with the feminine (the archetypal feminine, not the feminine gender) we might understand the nature of the Holy Spirit in new and possibly significant ways.

To come to this understanding more clearly, it might be helpful to consider the purely archetypal dimensions of "the feminine" and "the masculine." In very broad strokes, the archetypal masculine can be seen as: objective, following the letter of the law, intellectual, directive, selective and hierarchical; the feminine, on the other hand, can be seen as: personal, receptive, nurturing, related to the other, inclusive and non-hierarchical.

From an archetypal perspective, then, we can see that "the feminine" is emphasized in the qualities of the Holy Spirit and in the festivities of the cult. This may reflect the deeper roots of the Holy Spirit (from the early Christians) and may be one reason why the practices of the cult of the Holy Spirit in the Azores take the form they do: personal, receptive, nurturing, related to the other, inclusive and non-hierarchical.

Was this knowledge of the early Christians known to Queen Isabel, the founder and patroness of the celebrations of the Holy Spirit? She came from Aragon, Spain where another mystical text, The Zohar, had appeared in her lifetime, possibly while she was still in the Spanish court. It was a text that also saw the Holy Spirit as an expression of the divine feminine.

Next week we'll look at this together.

# 4. THE ZOHAR AND QUEEN ISABEL

In the last article, a radical point of view was proposed: the idea that the Holy Spirit is related to the feminine, most notably the archetypal feminine. Now let's take a step further, going from archetypal to divine, and then bring in Queen Isabel and the Celebration of the Holy Spirit. This is a longer article, so please bear with me.

In the Dead Sea Scrolls, and in the written Hebrew of the Old Testament as well, the Holy Spirit was referred to as *Ruach.* The Hebrew word, *Ruach,* is a noun of feminine gender. Thus, in the Old Testament language of the prophets, "She" is the divine sacred spirit of sanctification and creativity and is considered to be related to the feminine. These profound and revelatory discoveries of archaeology and ancient spiritual texts may point the way to the future (which we will talk about next week). It is becoming clear, then, in re-examining certain early Christian beliefs that Christianity was closer to the feminine spirit than we ever realized.

In Kabbalistic mystical texts, *Ruach,* or "presence of God," was also referred to as the *Shekinah.* As we will read, the *Shekinah* is also a divine feminine presence.

In the Book of Zohar (1290), a Kabbalistic mystical text, the image of the *Shekinah* was a tremendous revelation. Here was the lost feminine imagery of God as well as that of the Holy Spirit. Because the tradition of

Kabbalah recognizes the feminine aspect of the Godhead (referred to as Divine Wisdom and the Holy Spirit) it shows how the orthodoxy of Christianity had lost touch with the ancient belief of spirit as "a great web of life," a belief that reflects the central quality of the archetypal feminine. Most importantly, Christian orthodoxy lost the recognition that the divine was present in all life — every blade of grass, every cell of our bodies.

The fundamental teaching of Kabbalah was the doctrine of emanation, emanation being the flow of divine light into all dimensions of reality, until it ultimately brings our world into being. Through this teaching of emanation, the Kabbalah showed the Oneness or unity of all dimensions of reality. Through emanation, God was present in every particle of both the visible and invisible worlds. The aim of the Kabbalist was to unite the two worlds — the invisible, divine world with the manifest world. Unlike other religious traditions, Kabbalism did not reject the material realm but saw it filled with the light of divinity.

The Zohar, or Book of Splendor, which appeared in late 13th century Spain is the principal text of medieval Kabbalah. It speaks of the divine feminine, the *Shekinah,* as the Voice or Word of God, the Wisdom of God, the Compassion of God, the Active Presence of God. The Holy Spirit of Christian teachings also refers to the Holy Spirit, the Paraclete, in these terms. Both Holy Spirit and Shekinah were intermediaries between the mystery, the unknowable, and the material world of manifestation.

St. Isabel (1271-1336), Queen to King Denis of Portugal, was the daughter of Peter III of Aragon in Spain. It is my feeling that Queen Isabel must have known something of the mystical depths of the Holy Spirit, or the *Shekinah,* by way of the Book of Zohar. She would have been about 19 years old when it came to light. The Zohar as a written document first appeared in her homeland of northern Spain during her young adulthood. She was a member of the royal family with all the education and cosmopolitan exposure befitting a princess. Her understanding of the Zohar may very well have been an inspiration for establishing the Celebration of the Holy Spirit in Portugal.

Through her founding of the Celebration of the Holy Spirit, the presence of God was activated in the world. Each year, the meaning of the Holy Spirit is renewed, engaging once again in concrete acts of of love, faith, hope and charity, with individuals acting in concert for the common good. This active engagement is also the fundamental teaching of the Zohar.

The *Shekinah* as the Holy Spirit offers one of the most vivid and powerful images of the manifestation of the divine feminine in our world. It transmutes all creation into something to be loved, embraced, honored and celebrated. It shows us that all creation is the shining forth of the divine intelligence and love that dwells within it and has brought it into being.

The *Shekinah* as the Holy Spirit personifies the web of relationships, the web that is the invisible ground of all life. Scholars and scientists may study the different aspects of this web of life under different disciplines such as cosmology, biology and physics, but an image like the *Shekinah* and the Holy Spirit unifies this diversity. Above all, it invites a relationship with it as something that is alive, conscious and the very ground of our own consciousness. The Holy Spirit, the *Shekinah,* can be understood as the soul of the soil, the soul of the land which teaches us its sacred, life-sustaining secrets.

Can we hear these teachings? Do we know how to listen? Soon, I hope to suggest some ways in which that can happen.

But first, next week, a conclusion to these last four articles. (My gratitude goes to Anne Baring, Jungian analyst, for her description of the Shekinah in Chapter Three of her book, *The Dream of the Cosmos: A Quest for the Soul*, some of which is reproduced here with her permission.)

# 5. THE VOICE OF THE DOVE

As we observed in one of the previous articles, for both Christian and Kabbalistic mysticism the dove was seen as the emissary of the Holy Spirit. The mystical tradition of Kabbalah was itself called The Voice of the Dove. We also learned that both traditions understood the Holy Spirit to be the presence of the divine feminine.

Taking a leap of insight, might we conjecture, then, that the prophesied Age of the Holy Spirit would include the deep acknowledgment of the archetypal feminine, the reinstatement of the divine feminine in a world in balance and harmony? Might the presence and profound acknowledgment of the feminine be the next stage of our global evolution and development in consciousness?

Portuguese philosopher and writer, Agostinho da Silva (1906 - 1994) is noted to have said that the Azores and the Celebration of the Holy Spirit "keep a secret for the new world." (My thanks to Dr. Antonieta Costa from Terceira, Azores.)

Perhaps the "secret" da Silva speaks of is directly related to the feminine, and to what the feminine, both divine and archetypal, means for the possible furthering of humanity.

Perhaps da Silva was suggesting that the Age of the Holy Spirit—an age, as Fiore believed, where humankind has a direct relationship with the divine, a full experience of universal love, in a non-hierarchical world—is being held *in utero* within the Azorean Celebration of the Holy Spirit. Perhaps it is held within the soul of the Azorean soil, until humanity is ready to reinstate the feminine to the sacred place it held before it was eliminated in all but certain mystical traditions.

The particular *spiritus loci* (spirit of place), the particular soul of the soil that forms the Azores, may contain the recognition and return of the divine feminine as co-creatrix. It may signal the fuller return of respect for the common good and the honoring of all life, life as the physical, living embodiment of the divine on earth. (Indeed, the Kabbalists saw this physical realm as "the garment of God.")

Maybe this vision is what the voice of the dove whispers from the waves and mists of Azorean seas. Perhaps the voice of the dove speaks from the shifting and quaking at the convergence of the three tectonic plates upon which the Azores rests, where new life and new ground is continuously formed through the paradoxical yet necessary regenerative forces of death. It may be that the voice of the dove teaches us to surrender our smaller lives in service to something greater than ourselves, and we become willing and conscious caretakers for the ground of being, the web of life, the "garment of God," our beautiful planet and home.

Over the following weeks we will see how we might attune our bodies (our personal "garment of God") to meet these geo-physical energies, the secrets of the soil, and perhaps learn to hear The Voice of the Dove.

## 6. Azorean Soul

I share with you here an experience of my visit to São Miguel. It's a circuitous route. Please bear with me; it's more personal than you might initially think.

The Swiss psychiatrist (and mystic), C. G. Jung, once wrote, *"Every soil has its secret of which we carry an unconscious image in our souls."* Every soil, every land, expresses its secret through us, through the lives of the people that live upon the land. At the root of this idea is the understanding in mystical traditions that spirit and matter are not separate. They are one.

How might this phenomenon be explained on a scientific level? French physicist, Jean Charon, writes about the nature of matter in his book, *The Unknown Spirit*. He speaks a great deal about electrons. His work has lead us to the discovery that electrons exist in a space-time continuum where there is a memory of past events that continuously and endlessly empowers and enriches not only what we call our mind, but every single cell of our physical being, in the very electrons that combine to make up our bodies.

Additionally, he says electrons form the building blocks of *all* matter. All life is made up of electrons — the stone of earth, the bone of body, the gnarl of wood, the eye of newt. Furthermore, he says these electrons communicate with one another, learn from each other, whatever the distance and whatever the species — human, non-human and otherwise. Electrons are able to exchange informational or spiritual content (he uses these terms interchangeably) in the ever-continuous flow of life's evolution. He goes on to propose that the electron is the wordless link between all of life, the bridge to inter-species and pan-matter communication.

According to Charon, "As time flows, Spirit increases its order within each electron...The electron does not consider this constant…increase as an aim in itself, in other words, the *object* of evolution, but as a means of *discovering the objective* of evolution...Each electron is like ourselves: as it increases its memorized information, it begins to perceive a new objective and to mould its actions accordingly…That is why we can speak of the spiritual 'adventure' of the universe, since Spirit is choosing to exist through constantly increasing awareness."

And now, back to São Miguel, where I very recently visited the country village of my family home.

I am not sure what happens to me when I am in nature, in contact with the land, but I do feel that I am heard (as implied in Charon's ideas about the electron). However, it is not this "I" that is heard. And I do feel that I can hear something, but it is not this "I" that hears. It's in the cells.

It's the actual flesh of my body alerting me to deeper realities through pan-matter communication: electrons of one body — of air, tree, chair, stair, water or stone — communicating to the electrons of my own body, helping me make connections in new ways, enlivening a greater sense of eros. This happened…

I stood there, in front of the house where I was conceived (but flown off to America shortly after). In that moment, I understood that when I was conceived, the soul of the earth had called my own soul there, right there, just steps away from where I was standing. As I stood in front of the house, I heard the echo of that call in my body. I could unmistakenly hear the physical sound of the rush of my soul, swift and sure, reaching, longing to come into form, the form that I know as

who I now am. At that moment, I knew I was a child
of this soil, of the land's soul, and softly wept.

# CLOSING THOUGHTS

Although the topics approached in each chapter of *Corpus Anima* are varied, there is, as you can no doubt feel, a thread that runs throughout.

The main and constant element that unifies and binds is the movement toward making sacred all that we encounter, whether that be through the suffering of soul, expression of body, rootedness to land, connection with numen.

In making something sacred or holy we are making sacrifice, from the lesser to the greater. The word sacred is etymologically connected to the word sacrifice, from *sacer,* ("holy"). From a depth psychological perspective, the lesser ego bows in sacrifice and dies to the greater Unknown, to the unconscious. We integrate into our consciousness a greater awareness - spiritually, emotionally, psychologically. In Jung's words, *The secret is that only that which can destroy itself is truly alive.* (Jung 1968, par. 93) In this passage, he was suggesting that we can only be fully alive when we relinquish the smaller ego-place, when we let it "die," be "destroyed," "sacrificed," allowing something greater from the unconscious to come in, making us more truly alive, more whole. Every integration of the unconscious is a blow or a death to the ego, but the resulting growth is life-giving. Without this integration nothing changes. We ossify, harden, fossilize. Creativity stops.

This act of sacrifice requires courage. It also requires trust. We learn trust in being re-formed by the blows of life, seeing that we can recover (given enough grace) and be yet ever stronger. The strength becomes an instinctual strength, built into the cells; it is a strength that arises by not pulling back from suffering but by allowing the disintegration of smaller, egocentric things, thus bringing us into greater connection with cosmic and mystical truths.

Each chapter touches on this theme in its own unique way.

Sacrifice, making sacred, seems to be foundational for one of the most important and urgent situations needing to be addressed at this time in history. If we cannot surrender, if we cannot sacrifice, make whole and holy, if we cannot listen and follow the deepest impulses of authentic and uncontaminated knowing of instinctual life at physical and spiritual levels, we will not be able to find a way to continue life as we know it now on this planet.

At the foundation of all chapters in *Corpus Anima* is a call urging us to find a way to respect and honor all life, no matter what the form. To this end, I find it enormously encouraging that Pope Francis has just released, at the exact time of this writing, his Encyclical Letter *Laudato Si', of the Holy Father Francis, On Care for Our Common Home.*

Pope Francis reflects to us the cry of the world soul, the *anima mundi,* the embodied soul, the ensouled body, Sister and Mother Earth. At last, one strong, highly influential spiritual world leader has requested urgently that we hear Her, that we hear Her cry. This is a courageous act.

Pope Francis ends his Encyclical with a prayer, an excerpt of which follows.

### A Prayer for Our Earth

All-powerful God, you are present in the whole universe

and in the smallest of your creatures…

Help us to rescue the abandoned and forgotten of this earth, so precious in your eyes.

…Touch the hearts of those who look only for gain at the expense of the poor and the earth.

Teach us to discover the worth of each thing, to be filled with awe and contemplation, to recognize that we are profoundly united with every creature…. (Francis 2015, p. 178)

The Pope implores us to honor and respect all life. He urges us to sacrifice the smaller, personal and ego-centered needs for the greater good, to make sacred our lives, and all life, by recognizing our inextricable union with every creature on this earth, indeed with the earth itself.

No matter what the topic, no matter what the discipline—medicine, teaching, engineering, yoga, psychology, banking, the arts—we cannot ignore, deny or abandon our relationship with life, with all life, with the earth, our earth. It is our home. It is our Mother. It is all our relations.

As I was concluding *Corpus Anima* with these final thoughts, my mother was here with me at home for palliative care. I was her sole caretaker for almost six months. We were and had always been very close. During much of the time I was writing, in fact, she was but short weeks away from death. She died at 92 and led a very full and, I might venture to say, a considerably conscious life. As we reached the end of her life together, there was a poem that continued for days to return to me. The images in the poem were very strong...

* * *

About four or five days after her death, I had the courage to go into her room and look at her things. To my profound amazement, I found the same poem that had been continuously running through my mind. She had cut it out of a publication and had written, "for Cedrus," on the margin and placed it discreetly on her desk. She had left it there for me to find. It was just a little piece of paper, worn and tattered at the edges from wherever it had been kept for so long. I think she wanted it to be for me just at that time, at her death. Of course, I broke down and wept for a very long time. We had never talked about this poem:

> Do not stand at my grave and weep
> I am not there. I do not sleep.
> I am a thousand winds that blow.
> I am the diamond glints on snow.
> I am the sunlight on ripened grain.
> I am the gentle autumn rain.
> When you awaken in the morning's hush
> I am the swift uplifting rush
> Of quiet birds in circled flight.
> I am the soft stars that shine at night.
> Do not stand at my grave and cry;
> I am not there. I did not die. (Frye 1932/2015)

With this poem, I can't help but think that as we destroy our natural environment, we also destroy the connectedness to eros, to loved ones that are, as Mary Elizabeth Frye's words suggest, nature vivified. Native Americans refer to our natural environment and all the creatures in it as "our relations"—tree, hawk, stone, fire, air. The poem affirms this belief and seems to take one more step: that our personal relations are embedded in all of life—the winds, moonlight, the light that glints off snow, the rain, tree bark and butterflies. Nothing of the one who has left their human body is lost, it is enshrined in all of nature. It becomes and is nature. Nature surrounds us as the *anima mundi*, the world soul, and perhaps, too, by the souls of all our ancestors, all our loved ones, all our relations, and nurtures us as nature does—but only as long as we nurture it.

\* \* \*

My medical treatment of choice is acupuncture, or Traditional Chinese Medicine (TCM). My TCM doctor here in Zurich is from China. My mother and I had both gone to him for several years. He came to our home to attend to my mother on one occasion when she was very near death. He described what was happening to her, her dying, as ch'i (life energy or life force) dispersing, dispersing out into the cosmos. It would later amass again into another life form. He didn't say it specifically, but I can imagine the life force dispersing out and forming again into stone, wind, tree, into stars, raven, rose, into river and night sky…. This tradition, then, along with Frye's poem, the Pope's Encyclical and Native American beliefs, suggests that all life is connected and interwoven: at death, the human being as gathered ch'i, or life force, disperses back out again as ch'i into the cosmos, into nature, as nature itself.

When we do not honor all of life we impoverish ourselves, we do damage to and break the Wheel of Life (the title of the collection of images used in this book); as described by these traditions and perspectives, we break the cycle of life, the wheel or circle of amassing and dispersing life energy. The ensuing imbalance can lead us precipitously and directly to our destruction, as we are seeing now in the natural catastrophes steadily increasing.

Since my mother's death I have indeed wept, every day. I miss her immeasurably. It has been a shock and I suffer with deep mourning. But I know with time the suffering will soften, my heart will heal. My soul, my body, will connect with her once again through the awe and beauty of nature that is all around. Her love is in all these things and they will touch me every moment of every day, encouraging me to go on into life. As Pope Francis suggests in his Encyclical, I will be reminded as "Saint Francis of Assisi reminds us that our common home [nature, this earth] is like…a beautiful mother who opens her arms to embrace us…who sustains and governs us all." (Francis 2015, p. 178)

\* \* \*

One of several experiences I have had of her "appearing" after her death through nature bears mention here. It was my first outing into the deeper countryside, up in the mountains of Braunwald, a favorite place for both my mother and myself. Suddenly, I looked down at my hand. There was a very small black butterfly that had landed on the finger that bore the ring that was very dear to her. I had decided to wear it to keep her close. The butterfly stayed, and as the seconds passed I realized I felt something almost imperceptible touching the skin of my finger, again and again. As I looked closer, I saw it was the little proboscis of the butterfly extending out and pulling back over and over again, making contact with my skin each time. It felt like tiny little kisses, filled with the intent of loving embrace.

Although not necessarily exclusive to happening in the natural world, this experience happened in nature, through direct contact with nature. Is this connection with the natural world and other experiences of the Wheel of Life not worth protecting and passing onto generations that follow us? Is it not the most important thing we can now do, given our environmental situation? Many people think this is true. And now one of the world's great spiritual leaders has stepped up and proclaimed this in a letter, an Encyclical, a communication that is intended for his world-wide spiritual community, as well as to all communities beyond his own.

* * *

My mother had a dream only a few nights before she died. I call it The Old Man and the Book dream. She saw a very old man sitting and reading a book, an embellished book, a sacred book. As the old man read he became ecstatic, she said, full of joy. He turned to her and asked her to read it, offering her the same experience of ecstasy and pure joy. It was three in the morning when I went to her bedside with this dream still fresh in her mind. She was in a hypnagogic state, still in the dream and yet with me in the waking world. I asked her what she might read that would bring her the experience of such joy. She said being born into a family that was able to talk with each other and work things out in love and understanding, with compassion and ingenuity (her precise words). This, she said, would bring her the most joy and ecstatic connection with life.

I think if we were all able to do this we could protect the Wheel of Life, we could sacrifice lesser desires for greater ones, for the common good. We would learn again and again that life is whole, holy, and acknowledge it as such in all our actions. Her wish is especially relevant for the whole human family: to create a world of dialogue and diplomacy, to work things out with mutual care and concern rather than endless wars and hatred for the other.

*Corpus Anima* is offered in service to her desire - to talk, to share our deepest thoughts, and work things out in love and understanding. Her wish is worthy of a collective desire, to be held by us all. *Corpus Anima* offers a path of discourse for the family of humankind to work things out with compassion and ingenuity, an ingenuity that creates something sound and whole, using exactly what is, elements and ideas indigenous to the needs of the moment, taking the future and reverence for all life into account.

\* \* \*

Interestingly, but not surprisingly, in the early hours of the morning on what was to be one of her last days on earth, as I sat with her by her bed in her lucid delirium, she started to name all the people in the family, all her brothers and sisters, her nieces and nephews...all her relations. She said Ma was here (her mother) and asked if Pa were here with his musical instrument (it was a large and musical family). She asked if David were here (her younger brother who is still alive) and if he had brought his musical instrument.

It is this connection to her relations that unfolded so movingly in the last hours of her life and which remained so important at the hour of her death. Her response to the dream of The Old Man and the Book was coming alive as death approached. She wanted so much to be with them, in love and holy communion as her life was transmuting, as the life force was dispersing into the cosmos. It is my feeling from being with my mother until the moment of her last breath, and for almost three days after, that at the threshold between approaching death and preparing to enter new life, it is possible or perhaps inevitable that we experience the desire for this heightened connection and union with all those we have loved and who have loved us. We are nearly spirit at this stage, pure spirit, and it is to spirit that we are magnetized, the spirit that vivifies all life. This may be the critical stage that we enter, this communion with our personal relations, before we disperse into the cosmos itself, coming into union with all our greater relations - tree and stone, water and hawk, sunlight, starlight, the soil of the earth itself.

To make sacred all that we encounter, relinquishing the small self and attuning to the greater soul, the world soul, the *anima mundi*, to be in communion with all of life with respect, compassion and understanding is the "sacrifice" we need to make now together. Or as Pope Francis writes, "We require a new and universal solidarity." (Francis 2015, p. 13)

Pope Francis also writes, "…the divine and the human meet in the slightest detail in the seamless garment of God's creation, in the last speck of dust of our planet." (ibid, p. 9) To honor the life of the planet and all its inhabitants, sentient and non-sentient, is to honor the very act and fabric of creation itself; and it seems to be the only way we will survive on this planet at this time. *Corpus Anima* is offered as a collection of experiences and perspectives that attempts to show some of the many different ways we can perceive how the divine and the material are reflections of each other - how spirit and matter are inseparable and how living that understanding can make sacred all that we encounter.

*"…the divine and the human meet in the slightest detail in the seamless garment of God's creation, in the last speck of dust of our planet."* (ibid)

## REFERENCES

Jung, C.G. (1968) *Psychology and Alchemy. Volume 12. The Collected Works of C. G. Jung,* trans. R.F.C. Hull, Bollingen Series XX, Princeton, NJ: Princeton University Press.

Francis of Assisi. (1999) *Canticle of the Creatures, in Francis of Assisi: Early Documents, Vol. 1.* New York-London-Manila.

Francis, Pope, Encyclical: *Laudato Si', of the Holy Father Francis, On Care for Our Common Home,* 24 May 2015.

Frye, Mary Elizabeth. "Do Not Stand at My Grave and Weep," https://en.wikipedia.org/wiki/Do_Not_Stand_at_My_Grave_and_Weep (accessed on September 25, 2015 (original date of poem, 1932))

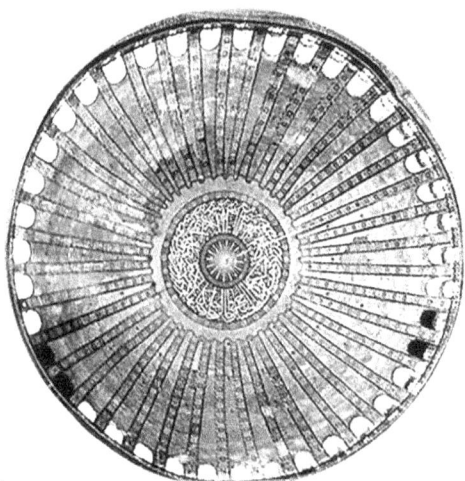

From the ceiling of the Hagia Sophia
(Church of Holy Wisdom) in Istanbul, Turkey

# ABOUT THE AUTHOR

**Cedrus Monte, PhD**, is a graduate of the C. G. Jung Institute in Zurich, Switzerland where she now resides. In addition to pursuing classical Jungian studies, her central concern has been exploration at the interface between spirit and matter, particularly as experienced through image-making (the arts); the psychodynamics of the body through movement; and cross-cultural spiritual disciplines, including Tibetan Buddhism and Native American traditions. She has received two generous grants from the Susan Bach Foundation (Zurich, Switzerland) which focuses on the interrelation between psyche and soma in conjunction with synchronistic phenomena. Present and developing interests include exploration of the individual psyche or soul in concert and connection with the world soul as experienced at the geo-physical level. For more information about her past activities please see www.cedrusmonte.org.

Cedrus Monte is a member of the Association of Graduate Analytical Psychologists (AGAP) and the International Association of Analytical Psychology (IAAP).

*9 7 8 1 6 3 0 5 1 3 6 5 8*